Hallissey!

A. Matthew Hufnal

DEDICATION

To my comrades past, present, and future, who serve and protect
Haverford Township.
…and to its residents, who make it a place worth protecting.

AUTHOR'S NOTE

The story that follows is true. As such, I have resisted the temptation to
arbitrarily add dialogue when it is clearly impossible to know exactly what
was said. Where quotes are used in the text, the dialogue contained therein
is lifted directly from contemporary accounts, with the attendant hope that
the original author was diligent in capturing it accurately. In those
instances where I imply a person's thoughts or motives, I have attempted to
consistently use qualifiers, such as, "…may have thought," or, "…likely
intended…" I sincerely hope the reader will forgive this literary device, as it
allows the story to flow more naturally.

As often as practicable, footnotes have been added to provide additional
information and sources. They can be found after the epilogue.

ACKNOWLEDGMENTS

Thank you to my wonderful wife and children, for tolerating (and then
encouraging) the Hallissey obsession that came out of nowhere and gripped
me for months. I am also very appreciative for the friends and co-workers
who listened to the stories, read the drafts, and provided me with
encouragement and feedback. These people are too numerous to
mention, but I trust they know who they are. Many can be found in the
Township Public Works and Administration offices, Police Department,
and the Historical Society. Thanks also to Chief Viola and Township
Manager Gentile—for trusting me. Finally, I would like to thank the
members of Chief Hallissey's extended family, who have been
understanding and supportive of my efforts. I doubt that I would have
proceeded to publish without their blessing. I like to think that Hallissey's
legacy belongs to all of us.

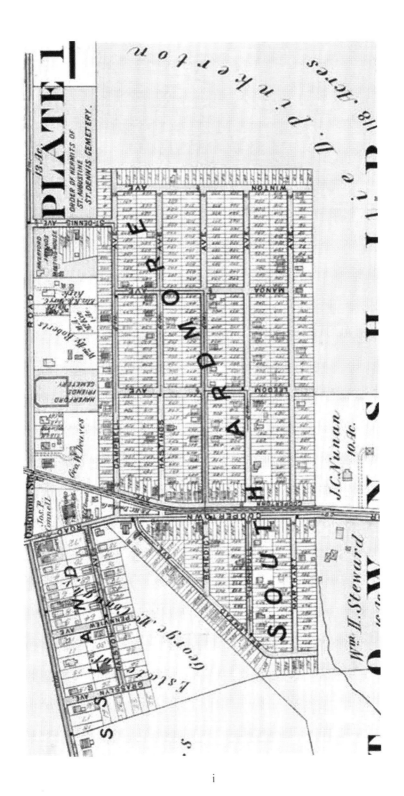

Prologue

In 1916, Haverford Township was at a crossroads in more ways than one. The heretofore sleepy suburb, perched on Philadelphia's western edge and home to under 6,000 people in its 10 square miles, seemed poised for great things. Its population was growing at a rate that would see it triple within a generation, and led by progressive commissioners like Horatio Gates Lloyd, the possibilities seemed limitless. A recent real estate assessment reported that the township had gained one million dollars in total value during each of the last three years, making Haverford the fifth-richest township in Pennsylvania. Although its western reaches consisted of remote areas dotted with farms, the northern half of the township held some of America's most valuable real estate--Main Line country estates of Philadelphia's elite. Horatio Gates Lloyd, perennially elected to head the board of commissioners, had recently completed the magnificent manor house of his sprawling "Allgates" estate on Coopertown Road. Designed by Wilson Eyre, the financier's 55-room mansion was surrounded by acres of manicured gardens made famous by his horticulturist wife, Mary Helen Wingate Lloyd. The Lloyds were philanthropists in the classic style, quietly donating millions to various campaigns for the common good.

Modern advancements, like electric lights, phones, and sewers, were incorporated into the new developments springing up in the growing towns of Llanerch, Brookline, South Ardmore, Oakmont, Penfield, Beechwood, Ardmore Park and Preston. Trolley lines connected the towns and allowed rapid transit between destinations from Philadelphia to West Chester. America's new fascination with "motoring" was well-supported by the commissioners' tireless efforts to improve the roadways of the township, and the tracks of the Pennsylvania Railroad's Newtown Square branch traversed the community. At Grassland freight station, near Eagle and Lawrence Roads, the Essential Oils Specialties Company increased their output of aromatic chemical extracts for use in perfumes and flavorings. Behind the long gray Essential Oils factory loomed the imposing complex of the Hall Concrete Company. Several buildings, totaling over 50,000 square feet, covered an area that would later gain infamy as home to the National Wood Preservers. The Hall Company, better known under their patented trade name of "Artcrete," had recently hit upon a winning recipe for the production of decorative urns, fountains, birdbaths, and benches. They were barely able to satisfy the country's demand for their pressed-concrete wonders. The factory was so large that it contained an internal tramway that passed through the 300-foot-long showroom, connecting the mixing and molding rooms to the loading docks of the freight siding. Dozens of workers in multiple shifts trundled back and forth along Eagle Road to the trolley stop at Oakmont. (1)

The township had passed a brief period of uncertainty in early 1916, when a committee of citizens in Llanerch considered seceding from Haverford and incorporating as a borough. "Llanerch Borough" would be bounded by Manoa Road to the north, Township Line to the south, Earlington Road to the east, and Naylor's Run Creek to the west. The committee explored their options, and learned that secession would require a court petition signed by a majority of Llanerch's residents. The movement lost steam, its leaders perhaps assuaged by the commissioners' solicitous efforts to convince the community that its value was fully appreciated. All involved decided to work through the differences over taxes and expenditures that had caused the brief rebellion, and indeed the entire exercise in civic amity had made the township stronger than ever.

Things were indeed going well for Haverford Township. The board of commissioners, incorporated just a few years before and made up of respected leaders who served out of a very real sense of civic duty, did all they could to promote the very idea of "progress." Laws were passed to regulate everything from the safe production of milk to the required fall-rates for a length of sanitary sewer (at least ¼ inch to the linear foot). A committee had recently been formed to explore the location of a new Township Building worthy of their modern community. The choices had been narrowed to two: a triangular plot of vacant land in Oakmont, and a parcel near the trolley stations at Ardmore Junction. The representatives of the Preston and Ardmore Park districts naturally preferred the Ardmore Junction location, which would best serve their constituents--who represented a sizeable portion of the township's population. In the end they deferred to the majority, and the Oakmont site won out. Soon, with an anticipated completion date in 1917, the township would no longer need to conduct business from a borrowed room in a Llanerch real estate office!

Forward-thinking leaders that they were, the commissioners had also recently formed a police committee. Their task was to research the ways and means to effectively implement the creation of a township police department. As realists, the commissioners recognized that crime has a way of keeping pace with progress. America in the early 20th century was a society in transition. Many previously rural populations, formerly with a small number of neighbors, were learning that crime might flourish in areas where everyone seems a stranger. Criminals naturally found that the roads and rails that made travel easier made their work easier, too. The system of having one or two elected constables and private citizens swearing out warrants before the local magistrate may have worked well for many years, but simply wouldn't serve as the population continued to grow. Also, the rise of the automobile introduced new concerns of traffic control and accident response. Growing towns were learning the lessons that the major cities had learned some generations before—that an organized professional police force is a very useful thing. The neighboring townships of Lower Merion and Upper Darby already had their police departments (instituted in 1900 and 1906 respectively), and of course the city of Philadelphia had been served by a large and capable department for generations. Nobody wanted Haverford Township to be seen as the soft hole in the middle, a target for crime pushed out of the neighboring communities.

And the last several years had certainly seen the township targeted. A 1911 burglary spree, of a scale and intensity likely not seen before or since, had shaken the community. A March 13th Philadelphia Inquirer article, headlined **"Thieves Terrorize Suburbs,"** reported that Haverford Township had endured 60 burglaries in a three-month period. It went on to state that although Upper Darby and Lower Merion had also been affected, "...Haverford residents have suffered most from the visits of burglars, because they lack a police force and have to rely upon one constable for protection." That constable, William Thompson, was clearly outnumbered and overmatched. He was even victimized—his motorcycle was stolen while he was investigating a burglary at the Eagle Hotel on West Chester Pike. The Inquirer described the crimes as committed by, "...one of the boldest gangs of burglars that has ever operated in this section of the country...Closets and drawers were thoroughly ransacked, carpets torn up, and even mattresses ripped open. Not a nook or corner of any house was overlooked in the search for valuables." Even farms were targeted, with the livestock slaughtered, dressed, and loaded onto the wagons, which were driven from the farms using horses taken from their stalls. George Deaves, an Oakmont builder and soon to be a township commissioner, discovered thieves had even entered his garage to strip his car of its wheels and metal fittings. "To attempt to give a list of all the robberies would be to present almost the [entire] directory of the residents of Haverford Township," stated the article with just the slightest bit of hyperbole. In addition to the burglaries, "yeggmen," or safe-crackers, were targeting banks and businesses. The Llanerch post office had its safe blown with nitro-glycerine at least eight times between 1910 and 1915. And twice within a few years, Constable Thompson was assaulted by prisoners bent on escape—both fleeing prisoners were stopped with shots to the back. Constable Thompson was even threatened by a gang of nude swimmers when he was tasked with breaking up the "disgraceful scenes" of regular "Sunday orgies" that had drawn complaints of rampant vice along the banks of Darby Creek. Although he was a capable and respected lawman, Constable Thompson held a full-time job with the Philadelphia and West Chester Traction Company. His constable duties were performed as a part-time elected position as an officer of the courts, and he could only do so much. (2) The State Police were requested to help with occasional patrols of the township, but they too were stretched thin. The time had clearly come for Haverford Township to have a police force of its own, and the first step was to select its chief. The commissioners searched for, and found, a respected man of action--a man that would mold a force in his own image. A man that would get results...

So it stood that in April 1916 Commissioner Samuel H. Moore, chair of the police committee, reported that they, "...have a man, highly recommended, who will come the first of May and organize a police force to be ready by June 1st." His terms, voted-on and accepted unanimously by the board, were $100 a month until October, whereupon his regular salary would be $125 per month.

They had found their man indeed, and that man was none other than the legendary Edward T. Hallissey.

THIEVES TERRORIZE SUBURBS; STATE POLICE ON GUARD

60 Robberies Committed in Haverford Township in 3 Months

RIDE UP TO HOMES IN AUTOMOBILES

Upper Darby and Lower Merion Also Suffer—Load Plunder Into Stolen Team

Robbed by burglars of silverware, jewelry and other valuables, representing thousands of dollars, during the last three months, residents of Haverford township, Delaware county, just across the city line at Sixty-third and Market streets, are now being guarded by the State Constabulary.

So daring became the operations of the robbers, who, according to the authorities of Haverford township, committed sixty robberies during the last three months, that a detail of the State police is now nightly patrolling the principal thoroughfares of Llanerch, Brookline, Grassland, Beachwood, Highland Park and other residential sections in the township. During the day the con-

A burglary spree of biblical proportion "terrorized" Haverford Township in 1911. The headline of this article, from the March 13th edition of the Philadelphia Inquirer, notes the "60 Robberies Committed in Haverford Township in 3 Months." The article goes on to assert that, "…Haverford residents have suffered most from the visits of burglars, because they lack a police force and have to rely upon one constable for protection." It's clear to see that in this environment, formation of a police department became a priority for the newly constituted Haverford Board of Commissioners.

Philadelphia Inquirer, March 13th 1911

OKOMSKY SHOT IN THE BACK

Runaway Prisoner Stopped With Bullet From Township Officer's Pistol

CONSTABLE W. F. THOMPSON

Special to The Inquirer.

LLANERCH, Pa., Aug. 4.—Constable William F. Thompson, of Haverford township, who has a reputation as a thief taker, was murderously assaulted this morning in Llanerch lockup by a man who is alleged to be a horse thief, but whose name is unknown.

The man had been captured while driving a team, claimed to be the property of Harry Pierson, of Brandywine Sum-

Endeavoring to escape from a constable who was taking him to the Ardmore police station, Peter Okomsky, of Third street, near Diamond, of Philadelphia, was shot yesterday by William Thompson, a constable of Haverford township. The prisoner was seriously, but not fatally injured, and after being treated was taken to Media jail. He was arrested on the charge of assaulting Mrs. Helen Gobrosky.

Okomsky met Mrs. Gobrosky in Philadelphia and insisted that she elope with him. The woman has a husband and four small children and she refused, but in spite of the refusal Okomsky accompanied her to this county. When Llanerch was reached the man again insisted that she elope with him, and her refusal resulted, it is alleged, in the man's attacking her, knocking her down and beating her in the face with a stone.

Mrs. Gobrosky is now at the home of A. J. McNally, Llanerch, in such a serious condition she is unable to tell

William Thompson, a court constable and Haverford's only lawman before the creation of the police department, had his hands full. These articles describe his battles with prisoners bent on escape, both of which ended with Thompson's judicious use of his sidearm. The first "murderous assault," as detailed in the August 5th 1911 Inquirer, began when a prisoner in Thompson's Llanerch Junction "lock-up" attacked him with an iron bar removed from a cot and hidden behind the prisoner's back.

Left: Philadelphia Inquirer, August 5th 1911

Right: Chester Times, February 22nd 1916

10

DISGRACEFUL SCENES.

Authorities of the County Endeavoring to Break Up Sunday Orgies.

For several Sundays past a number of disreputable men and women from Philadelphia have been conducting themselves in a most disgraceful manner along Darby creek on Haverford township. The conditions became so bad that the authorities were notified and an effort made to stop the nuisance and annoyance.

It is said that Constable William Thompson went to the scene of the disturbance two Sundays ago and that some of the men in the crowd threatened him. On Sunday a posse of constables from this county went to the scene, but the gang of men and women with questionable characters were evidently given the tip and everything was quiet. It is said that the men and women would bathe in the creek together in a nude condition and that their conduct and actions were most disgraceful. The authorities of this county are determined that such orgies shall cease.

This article details the type of "vice" complaints typical of the era: Philadelphia residents holding regular "Sunday Orgies" along the banks of Darby Creek: "It is said that the men and women would bathe in the creek together in a nude condition and that their conduct and actions were most disgraceful. The authorities of this county are determined that such orgies shall cease."

Chester Times, August 1st 1911

ROB LLANERCH AGAIN; LOOT WORTH $1100

For the "Umptieth" Time Marauders Arrive in Auto and Then Crack Postoffice Safe

Special to The Inquirer.

LLANERCH, Pa., March 27.—This town heard a dull, booming explosion shortly after 2 o'clock this morning. Then it heard five sharp reports of revolver shots. After that accustomed quiet descended upon Llanerch.

For the umptieth time, or something like that, burglars, believed to have ridden in and out of town in an automobile, broke into the postoffice, blew off the much-blown-off safe doors, and escaped with about $750 in money and enough stamps to bring the total loss to about $1100.

Llanerch is one of the most fashionable little post offices on the blue list of the Grand Fraternity of Burglars. It has been robbed so frequently in recent years that a feeling of ennui overcomes the people of the locality now when a robbery occurs.

The five revolver shots mentioned in the first paragraph were distributed toward the general direction of the post-

Any notion that Haverford Township of the early 20th century was a crime-free paradise is quickly disabused by even a casual review of newspapers of the era. Constable Thompson handled more than his share of robberies, burglaries, and assaults. This 1914 article sardonically states, "…Llanerch is one of the most fashionable little post offices on the blue list of the Grand Fraternity of Burglars. It has been robbed so frequently in recent years that a feeling of ennui overcomes the people of the locality now when a robbery occurs."

Philadelphia Inquirer, March 28th, 1914

A view of Llanerch Junction on West Chester Pike, circa 1915; looking west. The building with a covered porch near the trolley tracks was the station of the Philadelphia and West Chester Traction Company. Constable Thompson, a Special Police Officer for the company, maintained a lock-up inside this building. Behind it were the trolley company's "car barn" and power plant. The cylindrical water tower belonged to the Pennsylvania Railroad, whose tracks crossed West Chester Pike at this location (just west of West Chester Pike's intersection with Darby Road). Llanerch Junction, so named because it connected the Pennsylvania Railroad with trolley lines to West Chester and Ardmore, helped make Llanerch one of Philadelphia's most prominent suburbs.

Photo courtesy Haverford Township Historical Society.

Another view of Llanerch Junction, looking east on West Chester Pike towards Upper Darby and Philadelphia. A West Chester-bound trolley is visible in front of the station. This is currently the location of the Havertown Kohl's store.

Photo courtesy Haverford Township Historical Society.

WANT LLANERCH BOROUGH

Committee Plans to Secede From Haverford Township

Special to The Inquirer.

LLANERCH, Pa., March 9—Llanerch residents, who inhabit one of the most beautiful sections along the West Chester pike, want to secede from Haverford township and turn their community into a borough. Back of the movement is a declaration by a number of the men interested that Llanerch is not getting back enough in betterments for the amount of taxes it pays into the township treasury.

A local committee, headed by Henry V. Gummere, of Tenby road, and with Charles W. Michener, of Township Line road, as secretary, has been holding meetings for some time past and its members have been busy gathering data that will inform the citizens of Llanerch as to the desirability of the proposed change.

A brief secessionist movement roiled Llanerch in early 1916. Some members of the community, described as one of Philadelphia's most beautiful suburbs in articles of the period, felt their interests would be better served by incorporating as a borough. The section, served by two trolley lines and the Pennsylvania Railroad, was blessed with infrastructure, a strong commercial district at Darby Road and West Chester Pike, and large modern homes built on pleasant tree-lined streets. Above is a view of Darby Road looking north from Park Road, a block east of the Pennsylvania Railroad station.

Philadelphia Inquirer, Mar 10th 1916

Photo courtesy Haverford Township Historical Society.

Looking north across West Chester Pike, this view shows a steam train of the Pennsylvania Railroad on its approach to Llanerch station. The railroad allowed industry to flourish along its length between Llanerch and Grassland Stations in Haverford Township.

Photo courtesy Haverford Township Historical Society.

Chapter One

Edward T. Hallissey was born in hardscrabble Lynn, Massachusetts, on June 4th, 1883. His father worked as a "Morocco Dresser," meaning he treated and tanned the goatskin leather used in the manufacture of shoes. Lynn was known as the "Shoe Capitol of the World," and was home to dozens of factories that produced every kind of shoe. Hallissey's father Timothy had emigrated to the U.S from Ireland as a boy, while his mother Anna was a Massachusetts native. Edward was one of five children, and the family moved several times within the city of Lynn during his childhood. Edward grew to be an imposing man; broad-shouldered, well-built, and tall. He exuded military bearing, likely from his enlistment in the U.S. Army at age 17. He saw active service in Cuba, the American West and the Philippines War with the 13th and 7th Cavalry Regiments. Although the 7th Cavalry's most infamous battle, under the command of George Armstrong Custer at Little Bighorn, had been fought seven years before Hallissey's birth, it remained an elite unit tasked with difficult assignments. The Philippines War, a drawn-out affair following the Spanish-American War, involved a hard-fought jungle campaign against ferocious guerilla fighters. Hallissey was a capable soldier, and attained the rank of sergeant after several years of cavalry duty. He was well-respected by his comrades, and was toasted at a later Company H reunion as, "...a man of few words, but of action." While in his sixth year of service, Hallissey decided to leave the army and answered the call to be among the first recruits of the newly formed Pennsylvania State Police. The State Constabulary, as it was formally called, was the first of its kind in the nation. Created in 1905 in response to the rampant violence that marked labor strikes throughout the state in that era, the force soon proved its worth in policing farmland and industrial outposts in rural areas that had suddenly become hotbeds of activity due to large influxes of miners, steelmakers, and railroaders. These workers were rough men, used to handling things their own way; and without the need or care for police. Hallissey was equal to the task. He developed a reputation for fearlessness, and was sent to trouble-spots in 10 different counties from Philadelphia to Lackawana. He soon held the rank of Sergeant, and served as acting-Captain in Lebanon County.

In January of 1909, Hallissey was tasked with tracking notorious criminal Jacob Shell, who was on the run after shooting and seriously wounding State Trooper Earle Hollingsworth in North Annville Township. Trooper Hollingsworth had been shot through the face and thigh while attempting to serve an arrest warrant on Shell, who was determined to not be taken alive. Hallissey and his team tracked Shell on horse-back cross-country for three days before discovering him in the dining room of a hotel in Dauphin County. Hallissey spied Shell from across the room, his identification of the criminal no doubt helped by the fact that Shell had a pair of revolvers positioned on either side of his dinner plate. Shell was tired from his days on the run, and failed to immediately realize that the three serious men who had just entered the dining room were squarely focused on him. By the time he did notice the troopers, Hallissey was charging at him, revolver leveled directly at his face, and bellowing, "Put up your hands!" Shell, knowing that he was had, decided to give up after all. After cuffing Shell, Hallissey discovered that in addition to the two loaded revolvers, he had 40 rounds of ammunition in his pockets.

Less than a month later, Hallissey again made headlines for the arrest of Michael Loncar, variously described as a burly foreigner, desperate "Polander," or wild Hungarian. The reporters may not have been up to speed on Eastern European geography, but they were right about one thing—Loncar was a dangerous man. He had torn-up the barroom of Shirk's Hotel in a drunken rage, and stabbed the bartender who had tried to stop him. The Troop headquarters was some distance away, and Loncar had fled to the nearby foreign settlement by the time Hallissey and his partner got to Colebrook. They went house to house along the row of tenements before receiving a tip that Loncar was holed-up in a nearby attic. They entered the house and were met by more than a dozen hostile associates of the fugitive. Hallissey immediately bolted for the stairs, climbing several steps before they could attempt to block his way. He warned the belligerent men to back off, loudly repeating that he and his partner were State Troopers making a lawful arrest. Trooper Casner covered the group as Hallissey continued towards the attic. The men mocked the troopers, warning Hallissey that Loncar would not let him leave alive. Hallissey entered the attic and was able to grab hold of Loncar before the drunken felon could remove the folding knife from his pocket. Hallissey suddenly found himself locked in a desperate struggle for his life in the darkened confines of the cramped attic. Loncar refused to submit, and continued to battle for the knife. Hallissey thumped him several times with his blackjack, allowing him to finally get the cuffs on. He immediately dragged Loncar down the stairs and shoved him through the crowd of the thug's surprised confederates. The speed of the arrest had not allowed the group to form a consensus on what to do, but they continued to loudly discuss their options while following the troopers and their prisoner onto the road. Hallissey commandeered a passing flat-bed wagon, pushed Loncar onto it, and sat on his prisoner while maneuvering the wagon away from the angry crowd. The troopers retrieved their horses and bundled Loncar all the way back to Lebanon. Hallissey noticed that he was bleeding from several wounds; the attic fight had been so desperate that he could not recall if the injuries were sustained from Loncar's knife, boots, or hands. An addendum to one paper's account of the incident added the following: "Trooper Edward Hallissey, who for the past two months has been here, in command of the State Police, leaves on Monday to resume his duties at the Reading barracks. During his stay in Lebanon he has made many friends."

Hallissey's legend was secured a few months later, after details of his latest arrest were revealed in The Harrisburg Star-Independent in September 1909. The story, headlined "State Police Battle With A Desperado," involved a wild shoot-out that ended with the arrest of Israel Patterson, a career criminal who had terrorized the Carlisle area for months. The fact that Hallissey ended the gun-battle by putting a bullet through Patterson was almost incidental compared to what had led up to the confrontation. The term had not yet been invented, but Hallissey had gone into "deep cover" to bring Patterson to justice. Patterson had been robbing farms and businesses at will, tying up his victims and blowing safes at stops along the Pennsylvania Railroad. After each outrageous crime, Patterson disappeared into the thickly wooded mountains. The location of his lair was unknown to all except his fellow gang members, and it wasn't the type of place where nosy strangers would be welcome. Hallissey arrived in the area dressed as a tramp. He established his cover by living off the land and sleeping in the open. He panhandled and did itinerant farm work for ten hours a day to earn his food. He didn't fake it—he *was* a tramp. Day after day Hallissey bided his time. He befriended some fellow tramps but didn't ask questions—at least not right away. He seemed a likeable vagabond, and people wanted to know his story. Around campfires deep in the mountains, Hallissey told them just enough to make them believe he was a man looking to leave his past behind. The stories he told rang true, and soon he found his fellow tramps "opening up" with some tales of their own. Hallissey had to be extremely careful—if he was discovered in a lie, or was recognized by a criminal passing though the mountain camp, he would surely be killed by Patterson's ruthless men. After almost two weeks, he was accepted by Patterson and welcomed into the gang, befriended to the point that he found himself included in the planning for their next "job." Hallissey had what he needed. He knew Patterson's identity, his associates, and the locations of the camp and Patterson's shack. He had even discovered evidence of crimes in which the gang had not yet been implicated. The next day, Hallissey slipped away to find a phone in town. He called headquarters and told his men where to meet him. Their attempts to bring Patterson in peacefully failed when the old "yeggman" began shooting upon their approach. The troopers returned fire, hitting Patterson in the arm. A later account reads, "It was not until Hallissey fired a bullet into Patterson that the old man collapsed and gave in. He was taken to Carlisle and given the maximum penalty of 30 years in the Eastern Penitentiary."

A few weeks later, Hallissey survived a close call while attempting to arrest a transient bricklayer, Bernard Boyer, for attacking a woman in Wyomissing, Berks County. By the time Hallissey received the call, Boyer had disappeared into the darkness along the Lebanon Valley Railroad tracks, near the sprawling factory of the Reading Shale Brick Works. Boyer was waiting to hop a passing freight train, but Hallissey was on his trail before he would get the opportunity. As Hallissey moved in to make the arrest, Boyer attacked him with a hammer. Hallissey managed to fend off the first blows, but Boyer was a powerful man and pressed the attack until Hallissey drew and fired his revolver. The bullet passed through both of Boyer's thighs, instantly ending the assault. The bullet likely struck one or both of Boyer's femoral arteries, as he was near death by the time he reached Reading's Homeopathic Hospital. The hospital staff obtained a "dying declaration" from Boyer, who stated that he had attacked Hallissey in self-defense, claiming he didn't know the man chasing him was a police officer, and he feared that he was about to be robbed or killed.

And so it went...

Hallissey's exploits were splashed across the papers again and again. Hallissey gets his man deep in a coal mine. Hallissey arrests a double murderer, etc, etc. He was a household name—many of the headlines referred to him simply as "Hallissey." Not Edward Hallissey, not Trooper Hallissey, and not Detective Hallissey, which became his title after he quit the State Police and joined the Reading Police Department sometime in late 1911. What may be the quintessential Hallissey arrest story ends thusly: "...Chitshuck, who had taken his revolver to bed with him, fired as soon as the detective made his appearance, but, fortunately for Hallissey, missed his aim. Hallissey black-jacked his man into submission, and later obtained a complete confession."

Reporters, even in an age when hyperbole and embellishment were common tools to sell papers, recognized that their dispatches had the air of pulp fiction. Indeed, the most widely circulated account of Hallissey's heroics, syndicated nationwide in 1913, was titled "Real Dime Novel Detective." (3) Hallissey had become bigger than life. But cutting through the drama of contemporary accounts, the fact remains that Hallissey was a real person doing a real job. His job involved arresting dangerous men—and he was good at it.

At some point during his career with the State Police, Hallissey met and fell in love with Luella "Lulu" Bellman, who lived with her parents at 1513 Cotton Street on Reading's southeast side. They wed in March of 1907, and settled into their new home at 1557 Cotton Street, a stone's throw from Lulu's parents. Their pleasant little row-home was mid-block near the foot of Mount Penn; and from the back of the home Hallissey would have had a clear view of Reading's newest landmark, the fanciful 7-storey red brick "Shogun Castle" recently built on the mountain's south summit by eccentric businessman-politician William Witman. The Hallisseys began raising a family in Reading, but were struck by tragedy when their 4-month-old son, Joseph Edward, succumbed to illness in September of 1910. In a curious convention of the day, the same papers that had often carried stories of Trooper Hallissey's arrests ran obituaries that invited friends and family to call at his home address, where the child's funeral service was held. Pennsylvania's infant mortality rate was 150 infant deaths per 1000 births in 1910, a frighteningly high percentage that fortunately would soon begin to tumble due to rapid advances in medicine. It was around this time that Hallissey, perhaps eager to be able to spend more time with his wife and family, decided to leave the State Police and joined the Reading City force. The department at that time was without civil service protection, and served at the discretion of the mayor. This allowed the newly-elected Mayor Stratton to appoint him directly to the rank of detective.

Reading Pennsylvania of the early 20th century was a legitimate industrial metropolis. And Hallissey was in the thick of things. (4) The Reading reporters seemed pleased to have Hallissey working their city, but not all the news was good. In June of 1912, Hallissey had to stand trial as defendant in a case that Red Eagle Deerfoot (aka Roy E. Deerfoot), a Cherokee Indian from Oklahoma, had brought by swearing a citizen's complaint before a judge. Hallissey had been investigating reports that Deerfoot, a "lothario and panderer" according to contemporary accounts, had enticed a teenage girl to Reading in an effort to engage her in prostitution. Deerfoot alleged that Hallissey had brought him to the station without charges, and struck him twice on the jaw with his blackjack after Deerfoot balked at being placed into a cell. Deerfoot, acting as prosecutor, questioned the doctor who had treated him. Dr. DeLong testified about his "...broken right and left jaws, teeth and other injuries." Deerfoot's jaw was wired in two places. Hallissey was acquitted after offering testimony that his use of force was lawful and necessary. He perhaps felt vindicated when Deerfoot was charged with prostituting a different teenage girl in Lancaster in March of 1913. Testimony in that case supported the contention that Deerfoot was quick-tempered and violent: "The girl alleged that Deerfoot forced her on the streets and demanded all of the money that she earned, and that one night recently when she did not have as much cash as he thought she should have he administered a cruel beating to her at the corner of Market and Walnut streets." After reporting Deerfoot's loathsome activities in Lancaster, the Reading papers made sure to point out that he had been "run out" of Reading by Detective Hallissey.

In September 1913, the Reading Times reported that Hallissey was arrested while following-up a robbery case in another jurisdiction. The one paragraph story, glibly headlined **"Hallissey Held In Mahanoy City,"** reads as follows:

"Taking advantage of a day off to go to Mahanoy City to look up a robbery case, which occurred in Reading, Detective Hallissey was arrested at that place on Thursday in a bar room. A State Policeman with whom the local detective was not acquainted made the 'pinch.' He paid a fine before he was released from a charge of fighting."

In 1913, one would be hard-pressed to find a tougher town than Mahanoy City. A major rail-head for the booming anthracite mines of Schuylkill County, 16,000 people, mostly miners almost as hard as the coal they dug from the nearby mountain, were packed into the town's ½ square mile. It's a safe bet that most local scraps didn't merit the attention of the authorities, so one can only guess at the circumstances and scale of the dispute that landed an off-duty detective behind bars. There are no reports of whether Hallissey faced discipline for the barroom brawl, and the papers, usually so eager to recount his adventures, were decidedly mum on the issue. But to be fair, an objective observer would have to credit Hallissey for travelling to another city on a day off to follow-up a case on his own time.

"Extra! Extra! Read all about it!" In the summer of 1915, Hallissey was arrested in Reading and put on trial for Extortion and Bribery. The bombshell case, which gripped the city for months, devolved into a political circus involving the city's elected representatives and mayor. Notorious tenderloin criminal Tony Penn had alleged that he had paid "protection money" to Hallissey to prevent the arrest of Gussie High, a Reading prostitute and madam. Rumors immediately circulated that Hallissey's arrest was politically motivated in an effort to embarrass the mayor. Others speculated that the city's tenderloin operators orchestrated a frame-up to halt Hallissey's efforts to clean up vice in the city. The rumors of political malfeasance were so persistent, City Alderman Milton Kreider, who also served as the magistrate where the charges were initiated, felt compelled to publicly address the packed courtroom before Hallissey's preliminary hearing. Kreider denied that he was behind Hallissey's prosecution, or that he had knowledge that it was in any way politically motivated. The star witness, Tony Penn, publicly recanted his accusations immediately after providing his testimony. The District Attorney was tasked to investigate rumors that Hallissey had somehow coerced Penn to recant. A candidate for city council opposed to Mayor Stratton issued public demands that served to tarnish the reputations of Hallissey and the mayor. The candidate, Dr. Noack, wanted answers as to why Mayor Stratton had appointed Hallissey to the force in 1911, while at the same time knowing that Hallissey had been charged with an unrelated case of extortion while working as a private detective (he intimated that the fact that this earlier case was settled out of court proved Hallissey's guilt). Dr. Noack had joined the fray after a newspaper alleged that he had been named by Penn as one of the persons who had forced Penn to frame Hallissey under threat of arrest. Yes, it was all very confusing. Politicians on both sides threatened suits for slander. The drama culminated in a sidewalk confrontation between Hallissey and Fred Marks, a disgraced former officer who had worked in Hallissey's vice unit. Marks believed that Hallissey had sent an informant to City Hall to report him as a heroin addict. Marks was already suspected as being involved with instigating the case against Hallissey, and was fired. He confronted Hallissey inside a Penn Street restaurant, then waited for him outside. A crowd gathered as Marks screamed curses and threats at Hallissey, who replied, "If you're looking for trouble, I can give it to you." (5) Marks continued his tirade until Hallissey gripped him in an arm-lock, advising that he was under arrest for Disorderly Conduct. Marks howled in protest but could not break free. A crowd of "several hundred" people followed along as Hallissey frog-marched his prisoner more than three blocks to City Hall. The Disorderly Conduct case against Marks was dismissed with a warning from the judge, a minor side-note of the still-pending case against Hallissey. That matter dragged on for months, until Hallissey's ultimate acquittal in December of 1915. The court directed that the case be discharged due to Tony Penn's failure to provide evidence against him.

Although cleared of the serious charges that had been brought, Hallissey apparently recognized that he had no future in Reading.

Indeed, when Mayor Stratton lost the election, Hallissey found himself out of a job. He obtained a position as captain of the defense-plant security force at the DuPont powder works in Wilmington. A few months later, he stood before the Haverford Township board of Commissioners. As touted by Mr. Moore, he came "highly recommended," and was ready to form a police department from the ground up. Although it may seem like he had already lived a lifetime of service and adventure, Edward Hallissey was just 33 years old.

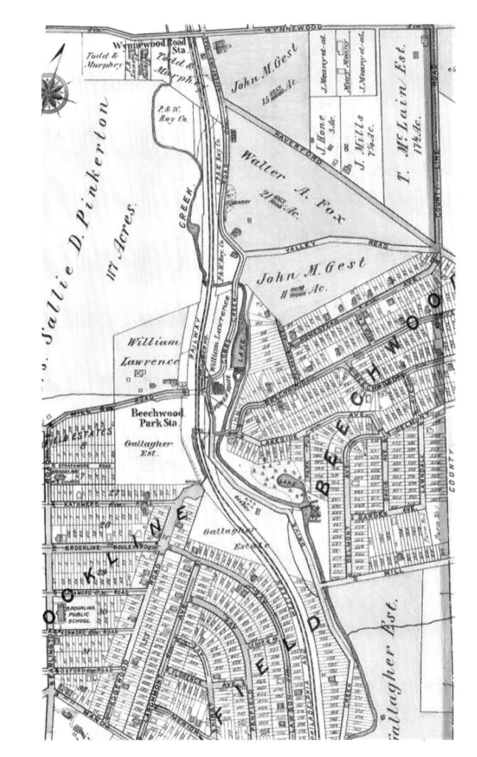

STATE POLICE BATTLE WITH A DESPERADO

Exciting Affair Ends in Carlisle Man's Arrest

FARMER ROBBED

When Troopers Tried to Arrest Suspect Fight Occurred

PATTERSON IS SHOT IN ARM

After Prisoner Had Been Wounded the Constabulary Subdued Him—One Bullet Passed Through a Trooper's Coat—Shooting Occurred in Carlisle This Morning—Patterson's Hiding Place Entered By Officer Disguised as a Tramp.

Special to the Star-Independent.

Carlisle, Sept. 29.—Clever and daring work of three State policemen landed in the Cumberland county jail this morning Israel Patterson, an ex-convict, who is held responsible for two robberies in the vicinity of Shippensburg recently.

Patterson was wounded in the arm in being captured and Harry Merryfield, one of the State troopers, narrowly escaped injury, a bullet passing through his coat.

Discovered Hiding Place.

Edward Hallissey, Harry Merryfield and Harvey J. Smith are the three State troopers who made the capture. Particularly dangerous work was done by Hallissey, who, disguised as a tramp, has been mingling with the gang of twenty or more desperadoes that have been habitating the district about Huntsdale for weeks terrorizing the country. Hallissey not only learned the location of Patterson's hiding place, but gained information about many other crimes that the gang has committed.

Risked His Life.

Hallissey came to Carlisle last Sunday and donned his disguise. Then he penetrated to the camping place of the gang of tramps and criminals about Huntsdale, in the southern part of the county.

Risking his life, he remained with the gang and soon learned that Patter-

HALLISEY KNEW THE PASS-WORDS

While Playing Tramp He Learned Patterson's Signs

How did Edward Hallissey get the range of Israel Patterson when the latter was at home?"

While playing "tramp," Hallissey had learned Patterson's pass-words. Such characters as Patterson keep under cover and that is why they are so hard to capture. They do not go in and out of their homes in the ordinary way, but are on the lookout for danger.

Mr. Hallissey had learned Patterson's pass-words on Monday. When

The story of Hallissey disguising himself as a tramp in order to infiltrate the mountain camp of a criminal gang captured the public's imagination and secured Hallissey's legend among Pennsylvania lawmen.

Left: Harrisburg Daily Independent, September 29th 1909

Above: Carlisle Evening Herald, September 30th 1909

ble
al-
or-
ne

the
fled
in
foll
job
sur
eho
he
He
for
he
to
wa
fell
ne
hea
his
the
wa
wh
an
wa
in
he
Alo
sha
ste
mir
dire
ing
H
wa
had
a
mo
kill
ter
and
we

Real Dime Novel Detective

SLEUTH THAT HAS HAD MANY THRILLING ENCOUNTERS WITH DESPERATE CRIMINALS.

[Philadelphia North American]

HALLISSEY was 30 years old Monday a week ago. So he has before him a future with plenty of room for more glory.

His work in Pensylvania has been done during the last seven years. For six years previously he was in the Seventh and Forty-ninth United States Cavalry, and he saw active service in the Philippines and in the West. He quit the Constabulary 18 months ago to do detective work in Reading.

Hallissey was a lad of 17 when he enlisted from his home in Lynn, Mass., at the close of his army service he had attained the rank of Sergeant. He was in California with his regiment when he learned that a state constabulary was about to be formed in Pennsylvania, and he wrote to Captain Groome for an appointment. He came to Philadephia for his final examinations, and was put on the "force."

He didn't know the meaning of fear. He was detailed on the more dangerous duties, and was finally made plainclothes man and assigned to all the big jobs that needed the services of a fearless man in Cumberland Lehigh Luzerne,

night back to Lebanon where he was tried and given nine years in the Eastern Penitentiary, for the wounded officers did not die.

This arrest made Hallissey a hero in the eyes of the farmers of Lebanon County. Testifying in Reading several years ago, when Hallissey had applied for a certificate as a private detective, Charles D. Weirick, the District Attorney of Lebanon County, said:

"A number of farmers came to me and said that, when the bill was passed and signed by the Governor, they were greatly prejudiced against the state constabulary, but, after seeing Hallissey's work they were strongly in favor of the constabulary, and felt amply protected when he was in their vicinity."

Hallissey distinguished himself again in Lebanon by his arrest of Michael Loncar, a Polander. Loncar was a desperate character. He had been in the Criminal Courts several times for making free use of his knife. His favorite drink was a mixture of beer and whisky, and after getting a good dose of it he went to Shirk's Hotel, and, being refused a drink, proceeded to smash the bar and break

This article, syndicated nationwide in July of 1913, summarized some of the highlights of Hallissey's career to that date. True to its headline, the facts may be slightly embellished; but most of the content can be verified by cross-referencing with other sources. The entire text of the article is printed in the appendix.

Washington Post, July 6th 1913

30

Center Street, Looking East, Mahanoy City, Pa.

In 1913, Mahanoy City was a booming coal town and major railhead for the anthracite mines of Schuylkill County. It was here that Detective Hallissey was arrested for a bar fight while following up a Reading robbery case on his day off. (Photo courtesy Mahanoy Area Historical Society)

HALLISSEY HELD IN MAHANOY CITY

Taking advantage of a day off to go to Mahanoy City to look up a robbery case, which occurred in Reading, Detective Hallissey was arrested at that place on Thursday in a bar room. A State Policeman with whom the local detective was not acquainted made the "pinch." He paid a fine before he was released from a charge of fighting.

Reading Times, September 6th 1913

Detective Leads Former Policeman to Lockup

Marks Said to Have Been Disorderly and Hallissey Puts Him Under Arrest

Another chapter to the feeling between former Patrolman Fred. Marks and City Detective Hallissey, which resulted in the dismissal of the former from the police department because of his rumored activity in a prosecution against Hallissey was added Thursday afternoon when Marks was arrested at Sixth and Penn streets by Hallissey on a charge of disorderly conduct.

The arrest and incidents leading up to created all sorts of excitement in the vicinity of Sixth and Penn streets, and a crowd of several hundred men and boys followed Hallissey and his prisoner to police station. City Clerk Charles Marks protested that his brother's arrest was spitework. Turnkey Richards ordered him to be quiet.

Live Session Today

A forfeit of $10 was placed for Marks' appearance at police court this morning by the city clerk, and the session promises to furnish the most lively doings that have occurred at City Hall for some time.

Flow of Language

Thursday afternoon about 4 o'clock Hallissey was seated in a Penn street restaurant when Marks entered and accused him of circulating a report that he (Marks) was "hitting the dope." There was an exchange of language.

Hallissey finished eating and left the restaurant. Outside Marks started—

(Turn to Page Three, Column Three)

DETECTIVE

(Continued from First Page.)

ed to curse the detective. Hallissey walked up Penn street to Sixth, and Marks followed, it is said, with fresh epithets.

Suddenly Hallissey grabbed Marks and started to lead him down Penn street. A crowd of men and boys, who were attracted by Marks' loud talk, followed in the wake of the pair and on the road the assemblage increased.

Alleged Disorderly Conduct

At City Hall the detective lodged a charge of disorderly conduct.

32

Left:

The prosecution of Hallissey for extortion, already the talk of Reading in 1915, took a spectacular turn when Fred Marks, a disgraced former officer who worked in Hallissey's vice unit, confronted him in a Penn Street restaurant. According to later testimony, Marks accused Hallissey of sending an informant to City Hall to report Marks as a heroin addict.   Marks, already under suspicion of instigating Hallissey's prosecution, was fired. Hallissey attempted to walk away from the confrontation, but Marks followed him up Penn Street screaming curses. Sidewalk gawkers were treated to the spectacle of Hallissey gripping Marks in an arm-lock and frog-marching him to City Hall, where he was booked for Disorderly Conduct.

Reading Times, October 22nd 1915

Reading Pennsylvania in 1910. Penn Street looking East towards Mount Penn. A thriving industry and the booming Reading Railroad made the city a bustling and progressive metropolis. Penn Street was the scene of many of Hallissey's Reading exploits. Note Reading's famous "Pagoda," newly constructed and visible here on the southern face of Mount Penn.

Photo courtesy Historical Society of Berks County.

Chapter Two

As promised by Mr. Moore in April, Edward Hallissey was present on May 1st 1916, tasked with organizing a police force to be ready by June. The board met in their temporary meeting room, in a building owned by the Taylor Real Estate Company near the intersection of West Chester Pike and Darby Road in Llanerch. The minutes of the commissioners' meeting do not record what was said by way of introductions, but they do show that Mr. Moore, as police committee chair, addressed the board:

"We ask the consent of the Board to adopt the civil service rules in the selection of our force, and that all applicants pass an examination as to physical and mental condition and knowledge of Rules and Regulation pertaining to the Bureau of Police.

We recommend suits made from sample 01041/2, costing $18.75 each, uniform to be like style 605 for the Chief and style 611 for the Force, caps same as style 605.

We recommend a pair each of plain trousers for use on special occasions, also to have an appropriate badge marked 'Haverford Township Bureau of Police', and to start force with Chief, Sergeant and four officers—men to be about 5 feet 8 inches, and to weigh about 165 pounds. As there will be several smaller details we ask that they be left with the Committee and Chief. We have estimated the cost of the above as follows:

Motor cycle, $250., four bicycles, $100., six suits, $240., Revolvers and equipment, $110., horse, $250., Ford Auto, $475., Hand Cuffs, $30., Rain Coats, $36., Office Furniture, $250., Saddle, etc., $20; Total, $1761."

The board unanimously voted to adopt the police committee's recommendations. In other business, they discussed a bond issue that would allow the township to pay for road paving with bituminous material. The highway committee had researched the costs associated with regular road maintenance, which until that time involved scraping the surface and laying hard cinders that were regularly delivered by railcar to the freight stations at Llanerch and Grassland. The issue passed, allowing the township to solicit bids for macadamized roads.

At the next meeting, on June 5th 1916, Chief Hallissey stood-by with anticipation. The board handled routine business—a resident requested road improvements in the neighborhood of Bon Air Farms, and the request was duly referred to the highway committee. Road Superintendant Shupert reported that during the month, he had repaired Haverford Road from the trolley to Ardmore Avenue, put stone on Mill Road, finished Ellis Road, covered Lorraine and part of Haverford Road with tarvia, repaired Creek Road and the Bridge over Cobbs Creek, and at present time was working on Brookline Boulevard. The township treasurer, G. Howard Leedom, issued his report. The finance committee went through the lengthy process of listing and approving payment of bills. Commissioner Dewees, for the highway committee, reported on the bids received for road paving—the board voted to accept the committee's recommendations in the selection of contractors. After more routine business, it was finally time...

Mr. Moore introduced Township Ordinance No. 77, "AN ORDINANCE TO ESTABLISH A NIGHT WATCH AND POLICE FORCE IN AND FOR THE TOWNSHIP OF HAVERFORD AND TO PRESCRIBE THE DUTIES OF THE SAME AND TO PROVIDE FOR THE SALARIES OF POLICE OFFICERS." The ordinance was adopted by unanimous vote of the board—Haverford Township had its police department. The board then immediately voted to appoint, "...the following men for police duty, if they pass examinations, subject to the Chief's approval: George T. Neely, Ardmore; William Compton, Llanerch; Harry Grove, Preston; John

Glackin, Preston; Eugene Graney, Oakmont." Chief Hallissey had his men.

Next, Ordinance No. 78 was passed, which authorized payment to purchase the plot of land in Oakmont for the new township building. It was, by any measure, a momentous night for Haverford Township. News of the new police department was carried on page 3 of the Philadelphia Inquirer on June 12th, in the "Main Line Notes" column, immediately below details for the upcoming commencement at Narberth High School. Below the list of Haverford's new officers was news that Llanerch's St. Andrew's Methodist Church, on the corner of Llandillo and Lansdowne Roads, had dedicated their large new organ.

Chief Hallissey hit the ground running. His first initiative was to improve safety by instituting speed limits along several important roads in the Township. "Run Slow--15 mph" signs were posted on Darby-Coopertown Road, Brookline Boulevard, and Ardmore Avenue. Hallissey publicized the enforcement efforts, telling an Inquirer reporter in August, "I believe in telling motorists in advance. I do not want to make arrests if I can avoid it, so I am giving the automobilists fair warning." The campaign was well-publicized, with multiple stories printed in Philadelphia, Delaware County, and Wilmington newspapers. The general impression of the articles was that Haverford Township should no longer be considered a "speedway," and the chief of its "new" police force meant business.

In September of 1916, Hallissey and his officers received their first public thanks; for efficiently handling parking and crowd control at the 1916 U.S. Amateur Golf Tournament at Merion. The event was a spectacular success, and marked the first of many USGA Championships to be held on the newly-opened East Course. Chick Evans won in a thrilling playoff, and "the boy wonder," 14 year-old Bobby Jones, made his national debut.

In early October, Chief Hallissey was notified that a gypsy caravan had taken-up residence in the wooded property at the edge of the old

Farwood estate, between Cobbs Creek and the West Overbrook P&W rail-station in the southeast corner of the township. The encampment numbered over 80 people, and they were apparently used to occupying space in Haverford Township without having to deal with any law-enforcement authority. They paid lip-service to Hallissey's order to "pass on," and he was surprised to return a few hours later to find the camp fully set-up, with dozens of tents sprouting along the creek-side. Hallissey responded by locating and arresting Peter Guy, who, according to an Inquirer article concerning the incident, was the "...king of the band." The gypsies quickly parlayed for the release of their leader, striking camp and moving on to the woods and fields on the Philadelphia side of the border. Guy was released with the understanding that he would not return to Hallissey's jurisdiction. The incident revealed a hallmark of Hallissey's tenure as chief—first, he gave fair warning in an effort to gain compliance, and then took swift action if the warning failed.

Hallissey and Lulu had settled into their new home on Ralston Avenue in Oakmont, a half-block from his soon-to-be-completed headquarters. They would eventually raise four children there—Mary, Ethel, Edward and William. Hallissey worked tirelessly to ensure that his department had everything it needed while waiting for the new building to be completed. (6) Any hopes the commissioners had that their initial equipment allowance of $1761 would last the year were soon dashed. Hallissey quickly determined that his Ford sedan was, "...not heavy enough for the work," and the commissioners approved the purchase of a big Chalmers sedan for $1110. His Ford was given to Mr. Shupert, the roads supervisor. Hallissey also received four prisoner-cells for the police's temporary quarters, at a cost of $465, and a Bell Telephone call box system that included 32 miles of wire and cost $805. In the days before radios, the call-box system was essential for police communications. A central switchboard at headquarters linked 20 boxes positioned at important locations throughout the Township. While walking their beats in the business districts and neighborhoods, officers would use the call-box to check-in at regular intervals and be advised of calls for service that had been received in their area. Should an officer make an arrest, they walked their prisoner to the nearest call-box to request a transport to headquarters. If that proved impossible, they would request a nearby resident to make the call from their home phone. If an emergency call was received at headquarters, the dispatcher could activate a bell signal at the nearest call-box, and the chief or sergeant would respond with whoever happened to be nearby.

Retention of officers was a persistent problem during the early days of the department. Month after month, the police committee's report to the board of commissioners included notices of resignations or dismissals, accompanied by recommendations for appointments to replace the departed officers. After seven months of operation, none of the original five men were still working for Hallissey (although one, Eugene Graney, did later re-join the force). Occasionally the committee's report included a reason for dismissal; usually either unauthorized absence, disobedience, or the cryptic catch-all, "conduct unbecoming an officer." It's a safe bet that Hallissey was not one to tolerate insubordination or malingering. The chief's efforts to recruit "the best" were hampered by the police committee's insistence that officers be residents of the township, and he lobbied the commissioners to change the requirement. Mr. Lloyd, president of the board of commissioners, later admitted the policy was a mistake, and Township Ordinance No. 90 eliminated the residency requirement of the earlier ordinance. Some men left because they were aware that better-paying jobs were available. Several times during Chief Hallissey's tenure, the police committee reported to the board that the officers had formally submitted requests for better pay. It would appear that the board was well-satisfied with the department's performance, as each request was honored. It also appears that Hallissey was popular with the rank and file—an Inquirer article from December 1916 reported that the men had surprised their chief with a piano lamp for Christmas. The size of the department also gradually increased under Chief Hallissey, and would grow to 12 men by 1920. (7)

Hallissey was everywhere—the hard-charging cavalryman led from the front. Recognizing that his was a small department still gaining police experience, he often took the lead on important jobs. One such case, early in Hallissey's career as chief, resulted in the type of widespread coverage that had made him a household name in many areas of the state. In December of 1916, a frantic Ardmore mother, Mrs. Tompkins of County Line Road, contacted Chief Hallissey to report that her teenage daughter had been abducted by a man that lured her with the promise of employment as a bookkeeper. The man, Albert Grant (aka Raymond Gardner) of Boston, had disappeared with the girl, leaving his infant son behind in the "temporary" care of the girl's mother. Hallissey tracked the pair to Reading and then Altoona, where he learned they had departed for Pittsburgh. Hallissey contacted the Pittsburgh police, who discovered the girl alone in a hotel room—Grant had fled. The girl later confessed that she was about to drink poison in a bid to end her life just before the police found her. Hallissey went to Pittsburgh and personally escorted her home to her mother. She confirmed that Grant had seduced her into fleeing with him, and she suspected he was still in Pittsburgh waiting for her. Acting on a hunch, Hallissey inserted an ad in the Pittsburgh papers, purporting to be from the girl and advising that she had gotten away from the police and stating where she could be reached by telegram. Sure enough, Grant took Hallissey's bait and wired that the girl should telegraph him in South Bend Indiana. Hallissey instructed the South Bend authorities to be on the alert for Grant, who would be in sometime for a telegram from the girl. He sent a telegram in the girl's name, which Grant later attempted to claim. South Bend authorities placed Grant in custody and notified Chief Hallissey, who departed for South Bend by train. Hallissey was lauded a hero upon his return to Haverford Township. The press of his former city of Reading was especially effusive, calling the girl's recovery, "...only one of the many notable feats of the former Reading detective since he assumed his duties as head of the police department in Haverford Township, an exclusive Philadelphia suburb."

In early 1917, rumors of a strange religious cult began circulating in Brookline. Thomas Pentz, a charismatic jewelry salesman, had recently moved to Brookline from the area of 16th and Master Streets in Philadelphia. Pentz dabbled in "psychic reading" and the occult, and was known as "The Great Father" by a group of young female followers intrigued by his teachings on "sexual problems" and strict vegetarianism. The Frazee family, also recently-moved to Brookline from Philadelphia, had apparently fallen under Pentz's spell, and joined his group known as "The Circle." The Frazees' eldest daughter, Marguerite (better known as Marjorie), had wedded Pentz in a "spiritual marriage" on February 25th 1917, and planned to join him in a "physical marriage" the next day. But on the day of the planned nuptials, the Lloyd family, neighbors to the Frazees in the 300 block of Oxford Road, were aghast to see Marjorie run from her home wearing a bloody night-gown and clutching a large bloody knife. She was chasing her pet collie, which she intended to offer as a "sacrifice." She was joined by her mother, Mrs. Frazee, who the Lloyds soon realized was also incoherent and acting as though under a spell. Fearing for their safety, the Lloyds made an urgent call to Chief Hallissey. Hallissey arrived and was horrified to find the Frazee women mutilating their deceased dog outside the Lloyds' home. Hallissey was able to secure the women in handcuffs, but they remained beyond reason and insisted that Marjorie was the reincarnation of Christ. They referred to the collie as St. Peter, and insisted that they be allowed to complete the ritual by slitting the throat of their husband and father, who was waiting for them in their house. Hallissey entered the Frazee home and was stunned to discover Calvin Frazee, a well-to-do realtor and respected member of the community, kneeling in the parlor with his neck exposed, patiently awaiting his fate. "In all my years of police work, I never have had such an experience," Hallissey later told a reporter. Mr. Frazee, who like his wife and daughter was apparently suffering a form of hysteria brought on by near-constant meditation, was convinced that Marjorie was Jesus Christ, and was despondent that their ceremony had been interrupted by the timely intervention of the chief. Hallissey immediately launched an investigation into the cult, and learned that Pentz was awaiting his bride in Philadelphia. Pentz returned to Haverford and was promptly arrested, but Hallissey was unable to link him to the actions of the Frazees. Doctors pronounced him "perfectly sane," and he was released with orders to stay out of Delaware County. Mrs. Frazee and her daughter, meanwhile, remained delusional and were committed to the Norristown State Asylum. Mr. Frazee passed the doctor's examination and was released from custody--he and his youngest daughter soon disappeared from public view. Predictably, Hallissey's interruption of a ritual human sacrifice in the "posh suburb" of Brookline proved irresistible to the press, and they peppered their stories with praise for the chief's quick action and resultant banishment of the cult from Haverford's borders.

Unfortunately, the township's attention soon turned from the bizarre to the tragic, and the tragedy occurred at the celebrated Allgates estate of the Horatio Gates Lloyd family. Philanthropists that they were, the Lloyds allowed public access to large portions of their property, which straddled Darby Road north of Marple Road. Especially beloved by local children was a lake that had been formed by damming a stream that traversed the property on the western half of the estate. It was a popular swimming spot on hot summer days, and the Lloyds kept several small boats tied to a wooden wharf at the edge of the lake. On March 25th 1917, six-year-old Joseph Cernowski fell into the lake while attempting to climb into one of the boats. His sister, eight-year-old Stella, heroically jumped into the lake in an effort to save her brother. The water near the dock was eight feet deep, and both Joseph and Stella quickly went under. The desperate cries of their four-year-old brother, who witnessed the entire tragedy from the edge of the lake, brought two men running to the scene: James Newman, a caretaker on the estate, and Howard Leedom, the Haverford Township treasurer who was on his way to visit Mr. Lloyd. The men pulled the children's lifeless bodies from the water, but their frantic attempts to revive them failed. Heartbreakingly, the mother of the children arrived at the scene before the police or coroner could remove them. The sight of her two oldest children lying lifeless on the bank caused her to throw herself into the lake in a bid to drown herself. Although she was quickly pulled to shore, she remained inconsolable and insisted that she would die there. A deeply shaken Mr. Lloyd ordered that the lake immediately be drained. His staff set to work breaking down the dam, and the lake quickly disappeared into history. (8)

In April of 1917, America's entry into the Great War raised the collective angst of Haverford's citizens. The population had already been made nervous by the unrelenting news of barbarities inflicted on each other by Europe's "civilized" nations; now they faced the prospect of seeing their loved ones join the fray, and the fear of spies and sedition roiled the home-front. On April 11th, a series of massive explosions at the Eddystone Ammunition Corporation, near the Delaware River just outside Chester, killed over 130 workers, mostly women and girls from throughout Delaware County and Philadelphia. Although a later inquest determined the catastrophe was likely the result of an errant spark igniting the explosive contents of the artillery shells being assembled in the plant, company officials labeled it sabotage, and two men were quickly arrested in connection with the blasts. The explosions were heard by most residents within a 15 mile radius, including Haverford Township. Nationwide, German-Americans, who made up the majority of the immigrant population, found themselves under both general suspicion and government-sponsored observation. Many of the "least assimilated," including native German-speakers, were subjected to loyalty tests to prove their patriotism. German-language newspapers closed, Germanic names were Americanized, and all things considered culturally-German fell under scrutiny. Sauerkraut manufacturers even renamed their product "liberty cabbage," as consumers refused to purchase anything associated in any way with the Kaiser's Germany. Government officials everywhere responded in various ways to protect industry and infrastructure, root-out potential spies and saboteurs, and calm their nervous constituents.

In that spirit, the Haverford Board of Commissioners voted to authorize the police committee to swear in, "...100 reserve policemen, who should be citizens of the Township and over 21 years of age; such reserve policemen to be subject to the call of the Township at the order of the Chief of Police for emergency duty. And resolved, that while actually employed under such call or calls such reserve policemen shall have the powers of Township policemen, provided that such reserve policemen shall not receive any compensation for services so performed." In addition to forming Haverford's Auxiliary Police, the commissioners extended the hours of the paid officers to ensure the township was adequately protected. They formalized the arrangement by passing legislation to increase the officers' pay by ten dollars a month during the "current emergency." When the commissioners learned that Chief Hallissey had registered for the draft, as was required by all men up to age 45, they passed a resolution to ask that the chief be exempted from active service as an indispensible local official. Several officers respectfully tendered their resignations in order to join the fight "over there," and the commissioners promised their positions were assured upon their safe return.

In July of 1917, operations at Hallissey's new headquarters in Oakmont were up and running. An Inquirer article about the new Haverford Township Building called it the, "...finest and best-equipped suburban police station near the city." A good-looking two-story square building with classical details, it was built from locally-quarried fieldstone across the trolley tracks from the nearby Haverford High School. The police department had its own entrance on the north side of the building and occupied most of the first floor; with township offices and the commissioners' meeting room occupying the remaining space. A large garage behind the building housed many of the township's growing assortment of vehicles and road-maintenance equipment. Soon, the building would be joined on its triangular plot of land by rows of stores and apartments on Darby and Eagle Roads. In a foreshadowing of events that would come to a head two years later, Chief Hallissey took the opportunity to issue a public warning that due to continued complaints of "vice" in the township, the department would be stepping up enforcement against "Spooners," the colloquial term used for couples "being familiar" in automobiles. The Inquirer decided to pass on Hallissey's warning in the form of a sarcastically written nautical-themed advisement:

"OAKMONT—Spooners ahoy! Look out for squalls in Haverford Township, abode of millionaires and suburbanites and Chief of Police Edward T. Hallissey, or you will find yourselves on a lee shore. The chief is carrying on a campaign against you and all your ilk. If you want to spoon under the silvery moon on Haverford Township roads you will have to pay for it, with the addition of a probable lodging in the new police station for the night."

Hallissey was no doubt less than thrilled to see his response to actual citizen complaints reduced to a joke. Regardless, the warning had been given, and subsequent events would show that he was serious about the message.

As the months passed by, residents were taking note of the good work being performed by Hallissey's officers. The image of uniformed patrolmen walking their beats had become a welcome sight, and the traffic enforcement efforts of the motorized patrols had tamed the roadways of the township. Chief Hallissey issued a monthly report of the department's activities at each commissioners' meeting, and news articles mentioned the resultant drop in crime. The commissioners' decisions to create a police force and appoint Chief Hallissey were surely paying dividends.

Hallissey was quick to share credit for his department's successes, and liked to publicly commend his officers when he recognized outstanding work. During the March 1918 commissioners' meeting, Mr. Moore, chairman of the police committee, read the following into the record:

Dear Sir:

I have the honor to respectfully report to you that on February 6th Officer Downey arrested Charles Benel on Brookline Blvd. about 12 o'clock [midnight] on suspicion. This arrest proved to be very important as after investigation we found that this man comes from New York City where he was convicted twice for burglary and sent to Almyra reformatory for a term of from two to ten years and was paroled after serving three years. He is now held in Media under $1,000 bail for carrying concealed deadly weapons. On March 4th an indictment was found against this man by the grand jury. When Officer Downey arrested this man he found a .32 calibre revolver and ten rounds of ammunition on him.

> Respectfully yours, Edward T. Hallissey, Chief of Police

A few months later, Mr. Moore read a similar letter from the chief, reporting, "...the arrest by Officer Jenkins, of a suspicious character who proved to be a notorious burglar, having robbed many houses in the vicinity and who had loot to the value of about $3,000 in his possession. The man, after threatening the officer with a revolver, submitted to arrest." After hearing the details, the board made a motion to, "...commend Officer Jenkins for his conduct and bravery, and move that he be granted a week's leave of absence, with full pay."

Both arrests were featured prominently in the local papers. In the latter case, Officer Jenkins had stopped a man hustling along Tenby Road in Llanerch carrying a heavy suitcase. The time of night and behavior of the man immediately aroused the officer's suspicions. When Jenkins began questioning the man about the suitcase, a tussle ensued and he struck the officer in the jaw with a revolver. He quickly gave up when Jenkins pulled his own gun and was about to shoot. The suitcase was discovered to contain jewelry, silverware, clothing, and two additional handguns, all taken that evening from three homes on nearby Llandillo Road. Hallissey worked to identify the crook, who gave him five different names. The chief eventually discovered his address in

Philadelphia, and a search of that apartment yielded several more suitcases full of items stolen from Haverford Township homes in the previous week. (9)   Few crimes are more insidious and difficult to solve than residential burglaries, and these kinds of results are exactly what the commissioners and residents were hoping for when the department was formed. Many still remembered the horrendous spree of burglaries that plagued the township just a few years prior, and were thankful that the results this time were very different.

Hallissey and his department were also developing a strong working relationship with the volunteer firefighters of the Haverford Township Bureau of Fire. Oakmont, Llanerch, and Brookline Fire Companies had all been formed in the years prior to the police department's creation, and Bon Air and Manoa Fire Companies would come into existence in the years thereafter.   The police and fire services shared a natural affinity due to their common missions as first responders, and several officers also served as fire volunteers. One of the first large-scale critical incidents involving all of Haverford's public servants occurred in the late summer of 1918. On September 16th, contractors using dynamite to excavate a site near West Chester Pike and Eagle Road accidentally ruptured the Springfield Water Company's 16-inch main. The resultant torrent flooded the area, and left most of the township without water. It would take more than a day to repair the damage and restore the water supply, and tragedy struck in the interim. In the early morning hours of September 17th, fire broke out in the wooden three-storey clubhouse building of the nearby Bon Air Country Club (since renamed the Llanerch Country Club). Four club employees, including maid Anna Davis and golf course superintendent Bill Furlong, were trapped in their quarters on the upper floors of the building. Firefighters from the three Haverford fire companies responded, but were unable to effectively battle the inferno due to the lack of water supply. Two of the trapped employees were able to save themselves by jumping from windows, but Furlong and Davis perished in the blaze. Every pumper truck in the region, including companies from Philadelphia and Upper Darby, responded to empty their tanks onto the fire, but their efforts were for naught. Hose lines were connected stretching across the golf course all the way to Upper Darby, but the mile-plus length of the supply line reduced the water pressure to a mere trickle. Police, firefighters, and neighbors all watched helplessly as the clubhouse burned completely to the ground. (10)

Tragedies like the fatal country club fire notwithstanding, Hallissey's tenure as chief was going well by any objective measure. In addition to the professional success he was fostering within Haverford, he was enjoying personal success as an influential member of the Pennsylvania Chiefs of Police Association. The recently-formed Chiefs Association was instrumental in pioneering advances in emerging technologies such as criminal identification and fingerprinting. Hallissey's ability to blend jocularity with seasoned experience made him a featured speaker at the association's conventions and meetings. At the national chief's convention of 1918 in Kansas City, Hallissey made news by challenging another chief, Nickolson of Oklahoma City, to a footrace. A Kansas paper reported that Chief Nickolson, who was, "…one of the live wires among the chiefs and was always pulling off jokes," accepted Hallissey's challenge, "…and coats and hats were thrown off." Observers assumed it was all for laughs, as Hallissey, at 200 pounds, was much larger and presumably slower than Nickolson. To their amazement, Hallissey's size belied his speed, and the race ended in a tie. Despite the undeniable successes being enjoyed by the chief and his new department, there were also times when Hallissey and his men were called to account…

The Penn House Hotel loomed over the intersection of Penn Street and Lancaster Pike in Bryn Mawr. The three-story landmark had a large bar on the lower-level; popular with main-liners in these days before prohibition. A brief fight at the bar between two men, McFadden and Burns, started a cascade of events that soon led to some public criticism of Hallissey's techniques. By the time Hallissey's men got to the hotel, McFadden had departed and Burns stated that it was "all over" and he wanted to go home. He later claimed that the police "induced" him to swear out an assault warrant against McFadden. Well enough, perhaps, except for what happened next--Hallissey's men went to serve the warrant at McFadden's residence. McFadden was a chauffeur who lived at "Redwood," the Cheswold Lane estate of Mrs. John B. Thayer. Although less than a mile from the Penn House, Redwood was in Lower Merion Township. Mrs. Thayer was a celebrated survivor of the Titanic disaster less than seven years prior. Her husband, a leading executive of the Pennsylvania Railroad, had famously refused to enter a lifeboat while women and children were still aboard the stricken liner. Mrs. Thayer was awakened at 3:00 a.m. by the commotion attendant to her driver being hauled away by police. She called Lower Merion's headquarters to demand answers, only to learn that they were completely in the dark as to what had occurred. The escapade predictably resulted in a furor, as one would be hard-pressed to find a more beloved public figure than the widow Thayer. Aside from the indignity suffered by her, crossing into another county without even the courtesy of a call to Lower Merion was a serious breach of professional and legal protocol. Questioned about the matter by friends of Mrs. Thayer, Hallissey called it a "private affair" that would be "fixed-up." The McFadden arrest became just one of a series of incidents that caused people in the surrounding communities to begin referring to Hallissey as the "Kaiser of Haverford," and the "Czar of the Main Line."

Hallissey convinced the board of commissioners of the need to enact an ordinance barring peddlers and junk-dealers from operating in the township without a license. The commissioners did so in June of 1918, perhaps unaware of the implications. Lancaster Pike was one of the most heavily traveled routes in the Philadelphia area, and it cuts across the northeast corner of Haverford Township for a distance little more than three short blocks. Hallissey and his men began arresting peddlers who were making their way along the stretch without licenses to operate. They were taken before Squire Robert Thomas of Bryn Mawr, one of Haverford Township's two magistrates, and fined heavily. The peddlers, who conducted business in the Lower Merion neighborhoods on either side of the Haverford "corner," were incredulous that they were expected to navigate a circuitous route around Hallissey's 500-

yard-long stretch of Lancaster Pike to avoid paying a fine. The solution, of course, was to purchase a license to operate in Haverford Township. While residents of other communities began questioning Hallissey's style, most citizens of Haverford Township appreciated his law-and-order methods that had undoubtedly reduced crime in their communities. In October of 1918, Judge Isaac Johnson, the President Judge of Delaware County, made a publicized tour of Hallissey's department. Mr. Moore later reported, "The judge remarked that the Building and Police Force were the best he had ever seen."

Perhaps from his experiences working undercover in the criminal camps near Carlisle, Hallissey had developed a deep distrust of "vagrants and idlers." The demobilization of millions of men after the end of the Great War, and the constricting economy that went with it, resulted in large numbers of "rootless" men who lacked the traditional ties to their home community. The romantic image of the wandering hobo notwithstanding, many saw it as a problem they expected Chief Hallissey to solve. Hallissey researched a law from 1876 that allowed a magistrate the right to sentence an "idle person" to the "workhouse" for six months to a year. Hallissey instructed his men to put the law into practice. In its first week, Hallissey's campaign sent 24 men to the county work farm. During an interview for the Philadelphia Evening Public Ledger, Hallissey stated, "...the superintendent [of the work house] told me he could use some men for the farms, and, anyhow, I am sick and tired of seeing this county overridden with bums. From now on I want to serve warning on these panhandlers to steer clear of this county." The reporter wrote of Hallissey's "...relentless campaign to rid Haverford Township of floaters and loafers." Hallissey gave the interview at Upper Darby's 69th Street Terminal, terminus for the Philadelphia and Western Railroad trolley that traverses the eastern part of Haverford Township. After the interview was concluded, the reporter witnessed as Hallissey rounded-up a nearby vagrant and marched him out of the station. "Nice specimen," said Hallissey, "...six months for this bird."

Another article, published in the Philadelphia Inquirer and the Conshohocken Recorder in February of 1919, reported that Haverford officers had instructions to, "...arrest every suspicious individual found within their border at unusual hours of the night." The article went on to state that, "...patrolmen under Edward T. Hallissey, chief of police of Haverford Township, have picked up 37 persons since February 1st who could not readily account for their presence in Haverford Township communities in the early morning hours. Of these, two have been identified as dangerous thieves and have been sent to jail." The paper goes on to praise similar efforts in Radnor and Lower Merion Townships, and notes that, "...crooks are beginning to realize that it is not good business to haunt Main Line roads late at night."

But beginning in 1919, persistent rumors began to circulate, accusing the Haverford Township Police of overzealous traffic enforcement in an effort to assess heavy fines. Hallissey, it was alleged, had promised the Haverford Commissioners that he could make the police department "self-sustaining." (11) In addition to his titles of "Kaiser" and "Czar," Hallissey added "Terror of Autoists" to his list of nicknames in the press. Auto clubs began to issue public warnings to their members to avoid Haverford Township for fear of being accosted. John Broomall, an attorney in Media, attested that he had been followed by a driver that repeatedly attempted to bait him into a race while he and his wife were travelling along West Chester Pike. The sedan repeatedly flashed its lights and pulled alongside, the popular convention at the time to indicate a driver's willingness to test the speed of their machine. Broomall refused to accept, as he had heard the admonitions to avoid displays of speed in Haverford. To his surprise, when he turned off the pike towards home, he realized the other driver was a Haverford police officer. The situation blew up after Patrolman Eugene Graney arrested a married couple, Mr. and Mrs. Brehm of Llanerch, for violating the township's Disorderly Conduct statute while driving along its roadways. Their crime was publicly hugging in a manner that might offend, and they were returned to the police station and detained. Publicity of the incident caused outrage, and the scandal grew exponentially (recall that the bench seats and lack of safety belts of that era made it easy, some would say natural, for a passenger to cuddle-up close to a driver). Investigating reporters spoke to other people who had been caught up in the dragnet, and discovered that unmarried couples traveling or parked at night had apparently been singled out with special vigor. Squire Thomas would assess high fines to unmarried couples, confident that they would pay the fine to avoid potential embarrassment by being identified as "Spooners." Thomas became ridiculed in the press as the "Spooners' Squire." A national publication of the time, Commerce and Finance, published a scathing editorial, reporting that Squire Thomas had a sliding scale of fines depending on what level of intimacy was alleged: Hugging (one arm), $5; Hugging (two arms), $10; Kiss, $25; Kiss (lingering), $50; Kiss and Hug, $75. Speculating reporters calculated the amounts collected in the scheme, and accused Thomas of getting rich from it (magistrates at the time retained a percentage of the collected fines as pay, and the Squire did live in a nice large home on Old Lancaster Road in Bryn Mawr).

Reporters hounded Chief Hallissey and Squire Thomas at their homes. The chief was nowhere to be seen, and the door went unanswered. The sight of his chief's hat resting on the porch rail convinced the reporter that Hallissey was inside, because he was known to never travel in the township without his full uniform and hat. The old squire (and his family) made the tactical error of debating reporters in the front yard, daring his enemies to try to prove any wrongdoing. The other township magistrate, Roy Blackburn, publicly condemned the "Fine-mill," as it was becoming known, and accused Hallissey of using Squire Thomas "for a tool." He claimed Hallissey intentionally avoided his court because he refused to go along with the scheme. A Sergeant Reichner of Lower Merion Police went on record to say he once had to intercede between Patrolman Graney and a car parked outside Graney's jurisdiction near County Line Road, telling a reporter that he warned the couple they were being spied upon and advised Graney to stay on his own side. Demands from the press and public became so great that County President-Judge Johnson recommended that those who felt wronged could file private suit against Hallissey and the Squire. Some critics demanded that District Attorney John Hannum file criminal charges against the pair—he investigated and declined to do so. William Schaffer, the state's Attorney General, also declined to get involved (a decision no doubt complicated by the fact that Schaffer had written the township's Disorderly Conduct ordinance while working as counsel for the board before serving as Attorney General). Members of the board of commissioners were blasted over the "Fine-mill" scandal during the summer of 1919, with petitioners repeatedly appearing before them and demanding that Hallissey be fired. Counter-petitions were submitted from residents supporting the chief. The commissioners promised an investigation, and subsequently announced that no action would be taken against Hallissey. Predictably, the papers called it a whitewash, and accused them of supporting the scheme because the collected fines benefitted the township. Through it all, Hallissey remained the picture of unruffled equanimity. When pressed for a quote on the matter, he replied simply, "You may say that as long as I am chief of police of Haverford, there will be no vice in the township." In Hallissey's police career, he had been assaulted, stabbed, shot-at, accused and arrested. This too, would pass. At the root of it, he stood accused of being overzealous in his duty, and he had certainly been accused of things worse than that. The reporters had done their best to find a smoking gun, but some admitted that the township's Disorderly Conduct statute, as written, made it impossible to find the department's actions wrongful. Hallissey would survive the scandal, the squire would not. Multiple candidates lined up to face him at election, any one of whom would have easily unseated him. Just before the election, the squire faced further disgrace when digging reporters discovered that in a previous legal dispute, the wife of a step-son, Emma Babb of Garrett Hill Radnor Township, had testified that the squire's true identity was John Pring Jacobs (other reports had it as Jacob Pring Jones), and claimed he had fled from England decades before, after being accused of embezzling village funds.

The very public sacrifice of Squire Thomas (and perhaps the less-publicized resignation of Patrolman Graney in September of 1919), must have served to satiate the public's demands for justice, for things slowly returned to normal. But in many ways the damage had been done. The negative and unrelenting press surrounding the scandal had likely shaken the board of commissioners, and Hallissey's name would be forever associated with the "Fine-mill." Little more than a year later, the bad publicity attendant to the affair would affect Hallissey in ways he likely could not have imagined. Meanwhile, he continued to capably lead a growing department tasked with protecting a flourishing community. The township's population was growing by leaps and bounds, and the commissioners were busy managing and directing that growth. Entire tracts of land were being developed at once. At the January 1920 commissioners' meeting, it was announced that the previous year had seen 70 homes built in the community of Brookline alone, 28 just on Brookline Boulevard. The commissioners were in the midst of crafting legislation that would allow them to borrow the astounding sum of a half-million dollars to complete the township-wide sewer system. They were determined to capitalize on the benefits such a system would bring their community, and legislated that every home and business was required to connect to the system as it went online street by torn-up street. The massive undertaking involved surveyors, solicitors, inspectors, contractors, developers, and representatives from neighboring townships and the city. (12) At the same time, previously private roads built as part of development tracts were inspected and accepted as public streets by the township. Each street needed to be surveyed and deeded to the township through legislation.

The fact that the police department under Hallissey was developing a reputation for professionalism and results is evidenced by the fact that in 1920, Hallissey was tasked with investigating two high-profile crimes in the neighboring communities of Broomall and Newtown Square. At that time, neither Marple nor Newtown Townships had police departments of their own, and Hallissey's reputation for always getting his man made him the choice of the District Attorney to handle the investigations. In the Broomall case, Clara Wolf, a young bride who had died suddenly on Christmas day of 1919, was suspected by her treating physician to have been poisoned. Mysteriously, Albert Wolf, who had only recently moved to Broomall with his new wife, disappeared after shipping her body away without obtaining a death certificate. Hallissey investigated Wolf's financial affairs, and discovered that he had gained financially from his wife's death. He also learned that Wolf was currently wanted in Albany New York for an embezzlement scheme he perpetrated immediately after leaving Broomall. The authorities in Albany suspected he had fled west. Hallissey traced Wolf's movements to Chicago and then Indianapolis. Hallissey had one of his men follow an associate of Wolf's to a Western Union office in Philadelphia, where he was seen wiring $3,500 to Wolf at the Hotel Claypole in Indianapolis. Hallissey obtained a murder warrant for Wolf, and characteristically departed for Indianapolis by train to return him to Delaware County.

In the Newtown Square case, a young lady named Pauline Culbertson was struck over the head with a lead pipe after exiting the West Chester Pike trolley at Barren Road. Her attacker fled into a nearby wooded area. Hallissey and his men arrived, and organized a posse of angry farmers who had responded to the area, "...armed with guns and clubs." The search lasted for three days over miles of ground, but unfortunately the man was not located.

By July of 1920, Chief Hallissey was favored to win election to the presidency of the Pennsylvania Chiefs of Police Association, of which he had become a high-profile member of the executive committee. As fate would have it, the association's convention in 1920 was held in Hallissey's old stomping grounds of Reading. While strolling along Reading's Penn Street and enjoying the company of friends, Hallissey's eye was caught by the sight of a distinctive and expensive auto that was approaching. His department had investigated the theft of a similar car just that week in Haverford Township. One of Hallissey's officers had obtained an arrest warrant for Michael Corcoran of Bewley Road in

Llanerch, who was suspected in up to 11 recent car thefts in the township. Sure enough, as the car passed him, Hallissey was able to clearly identify that Michael Corcoran was the driver. Hallissey ran to his car and followed Corcoran, who was unaware the chief was tailing him. Hallissey realized that Corcoran was heading southeast, towards the Philadelphia area, and decided that as long as Corcoran was headed in the right direction, he would bide his time in an effort to gather more evidence and possibly discover where Corcoran was taking the stolen cars. Corcoran stopped several times along the route. Each time, Hallissey stopped nearby and commandeered a phone to update his headquarters. Finally, Corcoran's journey ended at a garage in Norristown. Hallissey phoned his men to head to Norristown, then made the arrest. Five stolen cars were recovered, and Corcoran's brother Charles was also charged. The arrest had to be especially satisfying for Hallissey, for Michael Corcoran had attempted to discredit him in the papers during the previous summer. When reporters had put out the call to hear from victims of the "Fine-mill," Corcoran complained that Hallissey had attempted to shake him down over a speeding ticket. Strangely, no reporters seem to have picked up on the fact that one of Hallissey's loudest accusers and the notorious car thief were one and the same Michael Corcoran. Despite the glowing press he received for the improbable detection of a Llanerch car thief on Reading's Penn Street, Hallissey was not elected president of the chief's association at the convention. That honor went to Chief Tepel of Williamsport, where, perhaps coincidentally, the next year's convention would be held.

In October of 1920, a man by the name of George McGrath was appointed to the Haverford Police Department. He quickly proved to be an unreliable officer, and by November had been suspended by Hallissey for repeated instances of unauthorized absence. Before Hallissey could formalize his dismissal at the November commissioners' meeting, the appalling news broke that McGrath's real name was George McGinley, and he had just been arrested by Philadelphia detectives as a serial burglar. Details of McGinley's crimes were salacious and devastating. A partner in crime dressed "in drag" while committing burglaries with McGrath—they were apparently certain that an elegantly-gowned woman accompanied by a uniformed officer would be considered beyond suspicion. The pair had committed dozens of burglaries in the city and on the Main Line. Although it was obvious that McGinley/McGrath had joined the force for no other reason than to further his full-time career as a criminal, the headlines repeatedly referred to him as a Haverford Policeman by day, thief by night. No doubt resolved to minimize the damage to his force's reputation, Hallissey assisted the Philadelphia detectives in their investigation, and salvaged some positive press by personally arresting one of McGinley's accomplices, Frank Thompson, in the 69th Street Terminal. The curious case was followed closely in the news, especially when it was learned that McGinley had truly led a double life, with two wives, each unaware of the other, in different parts of the city. Bigamy was added to his list of crimes. McGinley was convicted and sentenced in January of 1921, and Hallissey worked to put the unfortunate episode behind him. Although he soon had a case that would occupy his time and attention, he had no way of knowing it would be his last.

On February 6th, 1921, Mr. Walter Pharo, of Panmure Road near Haverford College, discovered the bloody body of a man lying in a field near the Ardmore Avenue P&W station. He had been repeatedly stabbed in the throat, and his pockets were turned-out and empty. In one hand, he still clutched a fresh, half-eaten sandwich. With no I.D. on his victim, and no missing person reports that compared, Hallissey had a real mystery on his hands. He provided the press with as many details as he could—the victim looked to be in his mid-50's, with an appearance and style of dress that suggested he was an Italian laborer. Hallissey surmised that robbery was the motive. Within a few days, friends and neighbors of Pantalone DiCalla, of the 900 block of League Street in Philadelphia, contacted Hallissey to report they believed he was the unidentified victim. They travelled to the coroner's office in Lansdowne to confirm their fears, and told Hallissey that DiCalla, a laborer as the chief had guessed, was known to carry his entire savings, over $7,000.00 in cash and gold, wherever he went. He had left his home before sunrise on the day he was killed, on his way to a jobsite somewhere along the Main Line. The news that the brutal slaying was likely a targeted crime, and not the random work of a bloodthirsty fiend, may have somewhat quelled community fears, but it didn't make Hallissey's job any easier. He set to work researching everything he could about his victim. Hallissey knew the odds were good that someone associated in some way with DiCalla would prove to be the killer—relatives, friends, co-workers...all would have to be interviewed and investigated. History doesn't record if the Haverford Police ever got their man in the murder of Pantalone DiCalla; but if they did, Hallissey did not get the satisfaction of making the arrest. Fate had other plans for him...

The completion of Philadelphia's Market-Frankford elevated line to 69th Street Terminal in 1907 had created a rapid westward expansion of West Philadelphia's population. So it was that at about 3:30 p.m. on Thursday, April 7th of 1921, the busy Haddington commercial district at 60th and Market Streets was crowded with people enjoying a fine spring day. Shoppers competed for sidewalk space with homeward bound workers and students. Trolleys, automobiles, trucks and the occasional horse-drawn wagon navigated the busy intersection, while the rumble of trains overhead shook the stanchions of the elevated tracks. Assigned to help manage the traffic flow at this busy corner was Patrolman Grover Haase of the 61st and Thompson Streets station. (13) Officer Haase watched as a large sedan made a wide and sweeping left turn from eastbound Market Street onto North 60th Street. The car failed to properly complete the turn and drove up onto the sidewalk—the classic indication of a drunk driver. Curious pedestrians watched as a visibly intoxicated man exited the car as Patrolman Haase approached. The man wore a gray police uniform. It was Chief Edward T. Hallissey of the Haverford Township Police Department.

Eagle Road, as it appeared during Hallissey's time as chief. This view, looking east, shows the tracks of the Ardmore and Llanerch Street Railway crossing Eagle Road. The small structure in the right foreground is the Oakmont Station stop. The large home visible behind the station is the property of George Deaves. An outbuilding on Deaves's property served as the P.D.'s temporary quarters while the Township Building was under construction. The new building, which would have been directly to the right of this view, was completed in July of 1917. The large building on the left is the Haverford High School, completed in 1911.

Photo courtesy Haverford Township Historical Society.

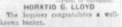

HORATIO G. LLOYD
The Inquirer congratulates a well-
known banker.

Horatio Gates Lloyd, financier and senior partner at both Drexel and Company and J.P. Morgan and Company, was the President of the Haverford Board of Commissioners during Hallissey's tenure as chief. These views show the front and rear of the manor house of Lloyd's "Allgates" estate shortly after its completion in 1912. Lloyd, a noted philanthropist known as "the father of jobless relief" in Philadelphia, was instrumental in both Hallissey's hiring and dismissal.

Philadelphia Inquirer, January 14th 1927. Photos courtesy Haverford Historical Society.

A view of the Allgates lake, formed by damming a stream on the western edge of the property. A wooden pier is visible in front of the log-cabin lake house. It was here that two local children drowned in March of 1917; H.G. Lloyd immediately ordered that the lake be drained, as their mother had thrown herself into the lake in a bid to drown herself. Ruins of the lake-house can still be found along the wooded trail north of Marple Road.

Photo courtesy Haverford Township Historical Society.

REGISTRATION CARD

| SERIAL NUMBER | | ORDER NUMBER | 1305 |

1 Edward Timothy Hallissey
(Middle name) (Last name)

2 PERMANENT HOME ADDRESS
30 Ralston Ave. Oakmont, Upper Darby Branch P.O. Penna.
(No.) (Street or R. F. D. No.) (City or town) (County) (State)

Age in Years	Date of Birth
3 35	4 June 4th 1883
	(Month) (Day) (Year)

RACE

White	Negro	Oriental	Indian
			Citizen	Noncitizen
5 ✓	6	7	8	9

U. S. CITIZEN			ALIEN	
Native Born	Naturalized	Citizen by Father's Naturalization Before Registrant's Majority	Declarant	Non-declarant
10 ✓	11	12	13	14

15 If not a citizen of the U. S., of what nation are you a citizen or subject?

| PRESENT OCCUPATION | EMPLOYER'S NAME |
| 16 Chief of Police | 17 Haverford Township |

18 PLACE OF EMPLOYMENT OR BUSINESS:
Haverford Township Bldg. Oakmont, Upper Darby Brch P.O. Penna.
(No.) (Street or R. F. D. No.) (City or town) (County) (State)

NEAREST RELATIVE
19 Name Mrs. Luella Hallissey (wife)
20 Address 30 Ralston Ave. Oakmont, Upper Darby Penna.
(No.) (Street or R. F. D. No.) (City or town) (County) (State)

I AFFIRM THAT I HAVE VERIFIED ABOVE ANSWERS AND THAT THEY ARE TRUE

P. M. G. O.
Form No. 1 (Red)
Edward Timothy Hallissey
(Registrant's signature or mark) (OVER)

Hallissey's Draft Registration Card. Hallissey registered for the draft during the uneasy period following America's entry into World War One. When the board of commissioners learned this, they voted to request he be exempted from any consideration of active service, as permitted for public officials under the Selective Service Act of 1917.

At the corner of Llandillo and Lansdowne Roads in Llanerch, the St. Andrew's church dedicated their new organ in June of 1916. News of the organ ran concurrently with the announcement of the newly-formed Haverford Township Police Department.

Photo credit Keith Lockhart, c/o Haverford Historical Society.

A view of Llandillo Road at Lansdowne Road in Llanerch. Two of the homes visible here were visited by the burglar arrested by Officer Jenkins in 1918. Postcard views such as these were used in real estate ads promoting Llanerch's large homes and pleasant tree-lined streets.

Photo credit Keith Lockhart, c/o Haverford Historical Society.

The Brookline home of Edna and James Lloyd, in the 300 block of Oxford Road (viewed from Pembroke Road). Hallissey responded here to a frantic call that two women were butchering their dog in the Lloyds' yard, and was credited with preventing a ritual human sacrifice in the "posh suburb."

Photo credit Wilbur Hall, c/o Haverford Historical society.

GIRL OF STRANGE CULT MEANT TO KILL FATHER

Police Chief Finds Her About to "Sacrifice" Parent Before Her Wedding

Parents of young women in Brookline, a Delaware County suburb, just west of the Sixty-ninth street terminal, are investigating, not without alarm, in their own families today to see if a strange preaching has pained influence.

A religious mania that made a great study of sex problems so influenced Mrs. Calvin Frazee and her twenty-two-year-old daughter, Marguerite, that they almost cut Mr. Frazee, husband and father, to death as "a sacrifice." Instead they "offered up" their pet dog.

When Chief Hallisey, of Haverford township, yesterday reached the Frazee home he found Mr. Frazee kneeling in the front room waiting to be killed. He told the police chief he believed his daughter to be the reincarnation of Jesus Christ.

Mrs. and Miss Frazee have been committed to the Norristown Asylum for the Insane.

If it had not been for the police interruption the daughter would probably

Predictably, Hallissey's timely prevention of a ritual human sacrifice by members of a "strange religious cult" was heavily covered by the press.

Philadelphia Evening Public Ledger, February 27th 1917

DRIVEN INSANE BY NEW CULT

Mother and Daughter of Haverford Township Crazed By Strange Teachings

Driven insane by the teachings of a new cult, Mrs. Calvin Frazee and her twenty-two-year-old daughter, Marguerite, of Brookline, Haverford township, were committed last night to the Norristown asylum, to which institution they will be taken today from the County Home at Lima. The police say this is the third case of the kind discovered in Brookline since Saturday and the Haverford township police are contemplating action against the teacher of the cult.

Mrs. Frazee is the wife of a former Republican politician of the Forty-fourth ward, an insurance broker, who recently moved from West Philadelphia to a beautiful home in this county.

Early yesterday Chief Hallissey, of Haverford township, was hurriedly summoned to the home of James Lloyd in Brookline across from the Frazee home. When he reached there he found a pet dog of the Frazee family with both ears off and bleeding from a gash on its nose.

Miss Marguerite Frazee, with knife in hand, had pursued the dog followed by her mother. When the chief had restored order in the Lloyd home he accompanied Mrs. Frazee and her daughter to their own house and found Mr. Frazee upon his knees on the floor quietly waiting to be killed.

Ordained to Kill Father

"In all my years of police work, I never have had such an experience," Chief Hallissey said last night. "I tried to reason with the members of the family, but they told me Marguerite was Jesus Christ and that she was ordained to sacrifice her father. The dog they believed to be St. Peter and they had decided to sacrifice it first."

(CONTINUED ON SECOND PAGE)

"In all my years of police work, I never have had such an experience," Hallissey said when describing the moment he found Calvin Frazee kneeling in his parlor waiting to be killed by his wife and daughter.

Chester Times, February 27th 1917

During Hallissey's tenure, residents became accustomed to reading positive stories regarding the work performed by the Haverford Township Police. Hallissey's "law and order" methods resulted in a significant drop in crime. Although some publicly criticized him as "overzealous," many community members rallied to support Hallissey when he found himself embroiled in the "Spooner's Squire Scandal."

Left: Philadelphia Inquirer, September 9th 1918

Right: Philadelphia Inquirer, February 17th 1919

HAVERFORD BAD SPOONING FIELD

Summer, Busy Season for 'Squire, Whose Fines Mount High

Heavy fines, ranging from $25 to $100, plus costs, which have been inflicted for years upon alleged "spooners" in automobiles in Haverford township, have paid for the maintenance of the township's modern police department and furnished a snug little income to Robert Thomas, justice of the peace, of Bryn Mawr.

If you were motoring along Lancaster pike, Ellis road, Township line road or any of the other highways in the township with your best girl, and the engine stalled suddenly or you had to fix a "blowout"—things began to happen. Though your halt may have been of a few minutes' duration, the chances were, nine out of ten, that you would be hauled into the little police station at Oakmont by one of Chief Edward P. Hallissey's ten men or maybe the chief himself. Half an hour later you were facing 'Squire Thomas, still dazed by the information that you were under charge of "disorderly conduct and immorality on the highway."

And "as sure as guns," to use the 'squire's own words, you "came across with the fine," with only the plea that it be "kept out of the papers."

But a monkey wrench has been thrown into the well-oiled machinery of the "fine mill," as it has been dubbed by the victims of the guardians of the law of Haverford township. This is the action brought against 'Squire Thomas by William Armstrong, of Philadelphia. Mr. Armstrong, through

STATE WILL NOT ACT IN SPOONING CASE

Attorney General Says Haverford Township Row Is Outside His Jurisdiction

DOZEN SUITS THREATENED

No action or investigation in the case of the alleged illegal arrest and "blackmail" fine system said to be conducted at Squire Thomas and the police force of Haverford township will be taken by William I. Schaffer, attorney general of Pennsylvania, according to his statement this morning. He said:

"I expect to take no official action in the matter, as it does not come within my jurisdiction. If the state should enter the case it would have to go to the district attorney and that is only in case there is a warrant sworn out against the "system" by one of the complainants.

"If the statements against the squire and his men are true, they could be brought to justice for conducting summary trials when a jury trial is called for," he continued, "and, moreover, it is grossly illegal to charge an offender 'for getting out of bed,' as it is said that Squire Thomas has done."

Hannum May Act

John R. Hannum, district attorney for Delaware county, may take up the case.

"At the present time I am not conducting any investigation," he said this morning, "but it is very probable that I shall before the end of the week. The only way in which I can officially conduct any legal prosecution is by acting upon a warrant sworn out by the complainants, but while none of them has done so yet, it is very likely that they will within a few days.

Negative press regarding the "Fine mill" a.k.a. "Spooner's Squire" scandal was unrelenting during the summer of 1919. Journalists were openly skeptical of Chief Hallissey and Squire Thomas, and questioned the motives of the Township Commissioners who unanimously voted to clear the chief of blame.

Left: Chester Times, July 11th 1919

Right: Philadelphia Evening Public Ledger, July 14th 1919

FINING SQUIRE'S VICTIMS DELAY TAKING ACTION

No Warrants Have Been Sworn as Yet Against Haverford Township Officials

Legal proceedings against 'Squire Robert Thomas and Chief of Police Edward T. Hallissey, of Haverford township, were at a standstill yesterday. District Attorney John B. Hannum, Jr., of Delaware county, when asked if any alleged victims of their "fine mill" had warrants issued, which would force the District Attorney to take action, answered in the negative.

In one case, Howard M. Lutz, counsel for William Armstrong, who claims to have been excessively fined by 'Squire Thomas, said that he would press the case to the limit. Mr. Lutz added that he had advised several of his client as to the proper procedure through which they could bring the 'Squire to justice, but as yet they had taken no action.

President Judge Isaac Johnson, of Delaware county, stated on Monday that those who allege they have been fined illegally that they could start action against Thomas and Chief of Police Hallissey by a simple procedure. By swearing out warrants against the two, he pointed out the District Attorney would be forced to investigate and prosecute.

HAVERFORD POLICE CHIEF ABSOLVED OF BLAME

Township Commissioners Hold Meeting and Unanimously Find Him Guiltless

Although demand was made that a probe of the police department be started to determine whether the charges of alleged illegal arrest and unwarranted fining of persons were true, the Board of Commissioners of Haverford township, Delaware county, unanimously adopted a report of its police committee which white-washed Chief of Police Edward T. Hallissey and his subordinates at a meeting held last night in the Town Hall, Oakmont.

No detail had been overlooked in arranging a proper background for the enactment of the little comedy of whitewashing the little but active police force. More than three score of Chief Hallissey's "friends" were on hand to see that "substantial justice" was done their much-maligned good friend. H. T. Burgess presented a petition signed by seventy-seven freeholders of the township, which indorsed the actions of Chief Hallisey.

There was but a single discordant note at the meeting. E. H. Bryant vigorously repeated his charge that he and his wife had been unwarrantedly arrested and later released after having been haled into the police court. He declared that former Policeman Flynn had given him reports of instances of illegal arrest and fining of persons who were guilty of no crime. He declared that the commissioners owed it to the good name of Haverford township to order a probe of the police force.

Horatio G. Lloyd, chairman of the

An Inquirer reporter, covering the meeting where the police committee carefully outlined their investigation before announcing their findings, wrote: "No detail had been overlooked in arranging a proper background for the little comedy of whitewashing the little but active police force."

Left: Philadelphia Inquirer, July 23rd 1919

Right: Philadelphia Inquirer, August 5th 1919

A 1920 commissioners' report announced 70 houses were constructed the previous year in Brookline, just one of Haverford's many growing communities. These homes in the 400 block of Kathmere Road would have been included in that total.

Photo credit Watts Real Estate, c/o Haverford Historical Society.

Now the site of a gas station and doughnut shop, the Penn House Hotel stood for many years at the corner of Penn Street and Lancaster Avenue in the Bryn Mawr section of Haverford Township. A controversial arrest following a fight at the downstairs bar led to public criticism of Hallissey's department from friends of Mrs. John B. Thayer, a celebrated survivor of the Titanic sinking.

Photo credit Lower Merion Historical Society.

IDLERS PUT AT FARM WORK IN HAVERFORD TOWNSHIP

Chief Hallisey Tells How Twenty-four Vagrants Have Been Handled in Week Under Old Law Recently Discovered

"We need 'em for farm work."

That was the answer given today by Chief of Police Edward T. Hallisey, of Haverford township, when he was asked to explain the inauguration of a relentless campaign to rid Haverford township of floaters and loafers.

Hallisey's campaign has been on for a week now, and in that time no less than twenty-four vagrants and idlers have been rounded up and sent to the workhouse for six months.

"We raked up an old law," said Chief Hallisey, "I believe it was the law of 1876, which gives a magistrate or a justice of the peace the right to sentence an idle person to the workhouse for six months or a year. The superintendent told me he could use some men for work on the farms, and, anyhow, I am sick and tired of seeing this county overridden with bums. From now on I want to serve warning on these panhandlers to steer clear of this county."

Chief Hallisey gave the interview in the Sixty-ninth street terminal, and after he had finished he excused himself. Within a few minutes he returned with a husky "weary willie." "Nice specimen," said Hallisey; "six months for this bird."

In 1920, Hallissey "...raked up an old law," that he claimed "...gives a magistrate or a justice of the peace the right to sentence an idle person to the workhouse for six months or a year." According to this article from the December 3rd Philadelphia Evening Public Ledger, Haverford Township Police sent "...no less than twenty-four vagrants and idlers" to the Delaware County workhouse in one week. It was this type of publicized enforcement efforts that had earned Hallissey the nickname "Kaiser of the Main Line."

Philadelphia Evening Public Ledger, December 3rd 1920

COP AND ROBBER

That Is Charge Preferred by Police Against Philadelphian.

(Special Telegram to The Enquirer.)

Philadelphia, Nov. 27.—A policeman by day and burglar by night is the dual role of George McGinley, alias "McGrath," according to the detectives who arrested him at his home. McGinley is a policeman in Haverford township, stationed at Oakmont. He is alleged to have worked with a partner, dressed as a woman, in robbing many houses in Llanerch and along the Main line, an is also charged with a number of hold-ups and robberies in this city.

McGinley lives with his bride of eight months at the address where Detectives Brown and Furguson arrested him. The woman told them it was not until his arrest that she found out that his name was not McGrath. She also said she had discovered a short time ago that her husband had another wife, living in South Philip street, with a four-year-old daughter.

The curious case of George McGinley, aka McGrath, "policeman by day—burglar by night," made national news and was no doubt a source of great embarassment to Chief Hallissey. He could not have known that this negative press would pale in comparison to the headlines announcing his own arrest months later.

Buffalo (NY) Enquirer, November 27th 1920

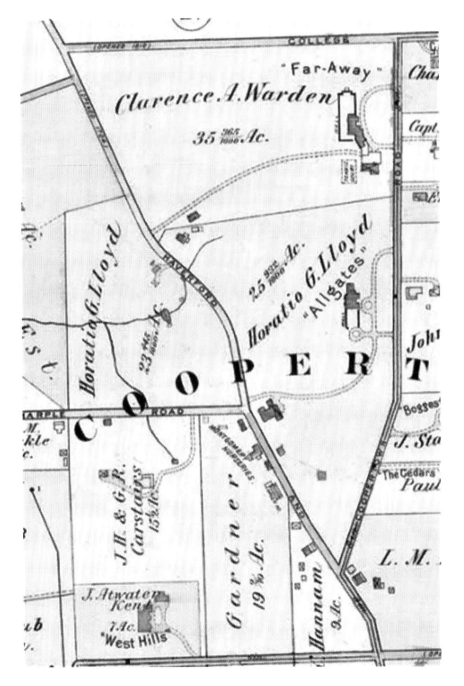

Chapter three

"What's the trouble?" asked Patrolman Haase as he stepped within a few feet of Hallissey.   His close observation of the chief served to confirm his original suspicion that Hallissey was intoxicated. "Nothing," replied Hallissey, and he turned back as if to re-enter his car; possibly hoping the sight of his uniform and his steady reply would serve to convince the officer there was nothing more to see. Haase interceded by guiding Hallissey away from the door and advising him that he would not let him leave. "Why not?" demanded Hallissey. Haase calmly explained that he was, "...not fit to drive." "Is that so? What are you going to do?" asked Hallissey. (14)

By now, both men were aware of the growing crowd of curious bystanders gathering around them. Haase attempted to reason with Hallissey, and told him that he was going to take him to the station house to let the lieutenant, "...sort it out." He began walking Hallissey north on 60th Street, towards a police call-box on Arch Street. Hallissey at first complied, but soon began imploring Haase to reconsider. "Officer, you seem like a good fellow....why not let me go?" Haase continued to guide him towards the call-box, and Hallissey's tone intensified. He told the patrolman, "My position won't allow me to be arrested. Let's talk this over in a reasonable way." Haase repeated that he would have to see the lieutenant. Hallissey became less cooperative, and seemed prepared to issue an ultimatum: "So, you intend to go through with it do you?"   Hallissey stopped walking and attempted to pull away from Haase. Then, in a voice steady and loud enough to be heard by several witnesses, he told Patrolman Haase, "...I'll croak you." Haase looked down and saw that Hallissey's right hand had gone into his coat pocket.   Hallissey was clutching his blackjack.

Patrolman Haase pulled his own blackjack, calmly advising the chief that, "...if you try any such thing...I'll croak *you*."   At that time, Patrolman Green, also from the 61st and Thompson Streets Station, was aboard a trolley traveling south on 60th Street, about to exit for his beat on Market Street. It's hard to imagine that he could have expected to be greeted by a more unlikely sight—Patrolman Haase, blackjack in hand, struggling with a uniformed police chief, and surrounded by a crowd of excited onlookers. Green jumped from the trolley and immediately grabbed Hallissey's right hand. He removed the blackjack and placed Hallissey into handcuffs. By this point, members of the crowd began to murmur, "...it's Hallissey!" Anxious now to get going, and still some distance from the nearest call-box, Haase and Green decided they would drive to the station house in Hallissey's own car. Haase bundled Hallissey into the back seat and climbed in after him. Green got behind the wheel and drove north on 60th Street. It was six long city blocks to 61st and Thompson, and most of the excited crowd ran all the way there.

The distance from 61st and Thompson Streets to the Haverford Township border is less than two and a half miles, so it didn't take long for word to reach Haverford that their police chief was sitting in a Philadelphia jail cell. Consternated friends of the chief immediately headed that way.

Meanwhile, Watch Commander Lieutenant Souder had summoned the commander of the West Philadelphia Division, Captain Smiley, to his station. He had also called for Police Surgeon Dr. Seabold. In the days before the scientific measure of blood alcohol level was developed, the professional opinion of a police surgeon was advisable to corroborate an officer's testimony. The lieutenant also gave orders to disperse the crowd that had gathered outside the station. The crowd removed themselves a respectful distance, but refused to quit the scene. The fact that the "Terror of the Main Line" himself was cooling his heels inside the jail electrified the crowd. Captain Smiley accompanied Dr. Seabold into Hallissey's cell, where they found him "dozing" on the bench. They awakened the chief, who immediately implored the captain to release him. History doesn't record the captain's personal feelings in the matter, but Hallissey had more than sealed his fate by threatening the life of a Philadelphia police officer on a busy sidewalk. Hallissey attempted to prove his sobriety to the doctor, extending his hands to show they didn't shake. He also asked the doctor to examine his eyes. The doctor immediately pronounced him as drunk.

A group of Hallissey's friends, led by Upper Darby Township Commissioner George Wadas, arrived at the station house by 5:30 p.m. They learned that Hallissey would not be released into their custody without bail. They asked for a copy of the charges, and set off to find a magistrate to arrange his release.

In a bizarre twist of fate, Hallissey was not the only chief arrested in that section of West Philadelphia on April 7th. A Sioux Indian, who called himself "Chief Rain-in-the-Face," had created a panic by riding a horse and firing blanks into the air as part of an ill-advised advertising campaign. He was corralled by the police and charged with discharging firearms within the city limits; he now occupied a cell next to Hallissey. When Commissioner Wadas and friends arrived with Hallissey's signed bail paperwork just after 8:00 p.m., the desk-sergeant called to the cell-block: "Release the Chief!" A few minutes later, Chief Rain-in-the-Face strolled from the cellblock into the lobby, "...bedecked," according to a contemporary account, "...in full war paint and feathers." "That's not Chief Hallissey!" exclaimed George Wadas, and then, with well-timed gallows humor, "...Or if it is, he's in awful shape!" Only then realizing the mix-up, the desk sergeant called for the "other" chief. Meanwhile, "Rain-in-the-face" took advantage of the confusion and walked out of the station--he failed to appear for his preliminary hearing.

Hallissey's friends managed to secure his freedom at about 8:30 p.m. He had spent four hours in a cell, and was told he would have to be back for a hearing at 7:00 a.m. the next day, Friday, April 8th. By that time, it seemed that everyone within 30 miles had heard of the incident. The courtroom was filled to overflowing, packed with reporters and bemused observers identified in the press as previous "victims" of the "Kaiser of Haverford." Contemporary accounts record that spectators cackled loudly and teased Hallissey, who clearly heard them say such things as, "...good for him," and, "...he deserves it." The papers noted that in contrast to his typical commanding uniformed persona, Hallissey stood silently at the hearing in a simple "sack suit," nervously scratching his right ear, shifting from one foot to the other, and twirling his soft brown hat. Magistrate Price played to the crowd—Hallissey visibly blushed and hung his head when Price repeatedly referred to him as a, "...country policeman." Officers Haase and Green testified about the incident, as did two civilian witnesses. The judge congratulated the officers, saying, "...This shows we have officers in the 29th District who always bring their man in when they go after him. These country policemen will learn to their sorrow that they can't monkey with the police of the 61st and Thompson Streets station house." Although apparently pleased with the patrolmen's actions, Magistrate Price became angry when Lieutenant Souder attempted to admit a brief summary of Dr. Seabold's findings in lieu of having the doctor present to testify. Price continued the hearing, scolding the prosecution that, "...just because a man had been drinking doesn't necessarily mean he's drunk." When asked by the judge if he wanted to speak in his defense, Hallissey nervously cleared his throat before answering, "I have nothing to say." James Robinson, the recently retired Superintendent of the Philadelphia Police Department, did speak on Hallissey's behalf, calling him, "...an excellent official who has never been in trouble before." Price responded that the evidence alone would guide his decisions. He announced that testimony would resume on Tuesday, April 12th, and ruled that Hallissey could remain free on the $1,000 bond. He also allowed Hallissey to claim his automobile, a request that had been denied the night before. On his way home after the hearing, Hallissey was approached by an Inquirer reporter. "...Nothing to say," was his first response, and then, with what the reporter described as a grimace that was half-smile,"...I got a tough break—that's all."

While Hallissey was attending his hearing on the morning after his arrest, the first articles detailing the incident were causing newspapers to sell-out fast. For the press of a news-hungry city that printed morning and evening editions, Hallissey was the gift that kept on giving. Friday morning's Inquirer carried news of Hallissey's arrest at the top of the front page, under a three-part headline:

"AUTOISTS' TERROR, MAIN LINE CHIEF, ARRESTED AS DRUNK—E.T. Hallissey Charged With Threat to 'Croak' Policeman—Official Noted for Strictness Accused of Running Car While Intoxicated"

Reporters were all over the story. In the few hours since the arrest, they had gleaned all the information from Officer Haase's report, and had interviewed witnesses who were at the scene. By the time the Friday evening papers were ready to print, they had added all the details from that morning's hearing. In the parlance of the day, the story "...had legs." By Saturday, it was national news. The April 9th Washington Times proclaimed:

"TERROR OF 'SPOONERS' LANDS IN POLICE NET"

Saturday's Baltimore Sun declared:

"'Auto Spooners' Terror is Himself in Toils—Haverford Police Chief Charged With Reckless Driving And Intoxication"

The Reading Times, whose readers were so familiar with Hallissey from his glory days in that city, felt particularly obliged to provide full coverage of Hallissey's spectacular fall from grace. Their Saturday feature story included Hallissey's picture under the following headline:

"E.T. HALLISSEY IN THE TOILS—Chief of Police, in Full Uniform, Arrested in Philadelphia for Drunkenness"

Reporters descended on Haverford Township in search of a scoop. Commissioner Dewees, of the police committee, attempted to be even-handed in his responses to reporters' questions, but admitted that if the charges against him were proven, "...Hallissey must go." Virtually all of the stories concerning Hallissey's arrest included mentions of the "Fine-mill" or "Spooners' Squire" articles from little more than a year prior. It was, of course, an irresistible premise: A by-the-book police chief known for over-enforcement of "petty" offenses is himself charged with drunken driving and threatening an officer. Today it would be called "Karma," but the oft-used phrase in the press coverage of the day was, "poetic justice."

The news had hit Haverford Township like a bomb. The board of commissioners scrambled to keep ahead of the story, and scheduled a meeting of the police committee for Friday morning. The committee met in Oakmont while Hallissey's hearing was being conducted a few miles away at 61st and Thompson. Commissioner Moore was in California, so the meeting consisted of just Commissioners Lloyd and Dewees. They quickly issued a statement that Hallissey was suspended, pending further action by the full board to be determined at an emergency meeting to be scheduled shortly. When told of the suspension, Hallissey advised Mr. Lloyd that his resignation was at his disposal. Commissioner Dewees met Hallissey outside his home later on the 8th, and told Hallissey he had just one question, and Hallissey could answer it or not, "...as he saw fit." Mr. Dewees asked, "Are the charges that the newspapers have made against you for this Philadelphia affair true?" Hallissey's reply was nothing if not admirably succinct: "I am guilty." Later that day, he delivered a resignation letter to headquarters, with a request that it be delivered to Mr. Dewees of the police committee. On Sunday the 10th, Hallissey was contacted by Mr. Lloyd, president of the board of commissioners, by phone. Mr. Lloyd advised him that the emergency board meeting would be held on Monday the 11th. He recalled his earlier conversation with Hallissey concerning his resignation, but hinted that some board members were not in favor of allowing him to resign—meaning they favored an outright dismissal.   Later on Sunday, Hallissey called Mr. Lloyd and stated that after discussing the matter with his wife, he considered the idea of resigning his position to be, "...a sign of weakness." He asked that his previous offer to resign be rescinded, and wrote a formal letter advising the same.

In an unfortunate case of bad timing, Hallissey was due to testify at the Media courthouse on Monday morning, April 11th. He was to be the "star witness" in the trial of Llanerch car thieves Charles and Michael Corcoran.   Many no doubt wondered if the suspended chief would appear.   He did, and according to the Philadelphia Public Ledger, "carried a broad smile" as he approached the courthouse and saw a group of friends there to greet him. He shook their hands and thanked them for the well-wishes, but said, "...not a word, there has been too much said already," when questioned by reporters about his arrest four days prior.   His appearance turned out to be unnecessary, as the Corcorans' trial was continued due to Judge McCullen's illness. Hallissey returned to Ralston Avenue to await his fate. (15)

At 5:00 p.m. on April 11th, the emergency meeting of the Haverford Township Board of Commissioners, "...to take action on the alleged misconduct of Chief Hallissey," was called to order.   Sgt. Loane, appointed acting-chief when the suspension was announced, occupied the chair usually filled by Hallissey, who was not in attendance. The meeting room was packed wall-to-wall, and immediately after the roll-call, Mr. Peter Gray of Brookline stepped forward to address the board. He advised the board that he carried a petition signed by over 500 residents of the Township, asking the commissioners to, "...favorably consider the reinstatement of Chief of Police Edward T. Hallissey, at the present time under suspension."   The petition went on to mention, "...his past favorable record, and the fact that his zealous performance of his duties had been the means of keeping this township practically free from crime." The petition was received and ordered filed. Other residents respectfully asked the board to delay considering the matter at least until the completion of Hallissey's Philadelphia hearing, scheduled to resume the next day. Mr. Lloyd acknowledged the crowd that had come in support of Hallissey, and advised them that the chief's past service and record had been given "serious consideration," but advised that the meeting would proceed to a resolution. Mr. Lloyd then recounted the meeting of the police committee, and recalled Hallissey's admission of guilt to Mr. Dewees. He mentioned Hallissey's offer to resign, and then the recall of the offer, stating that Hallissey considered resignation to be, "...a sign of weakness." He directed the board secretary, H. A. Fritschman, to read into the record both of the letters written to the board by Hallissey, first:

"Board of Commissioners, Haverford Township

Gentlemen: I hereby respectfully tender my resignation as Chief of Police of Haverford Township, same to take effect at your convenience. I also wish to take this opportunity in thanking the gentlemen of the Board of Commissioners very kindly for all favors bestowed upon me in the past, and I am certain that our relations have been most cordial. Respectfully submitted, (signed) Edward T. Hallissey"

And then,

"Board of Commissioners, Haverford Township

Gentlemen: Confirming telephone conversation of this date, with Mr. Horatio Lloyd, I wish to state that it is not my intention of resigning the position of Chief of Police at this time and desire to recall the resignation in your hands before any action is taken on same. Respectfully yours, (signed) Edward T. Hallissey, Chief of Police, April 10, 1921"

Mr. Lloyd expressed his opinion that Mr. Hallissey's actions amounted to conduct unbecoming an officer, and that since he had seen fit to recall his voluntary resignation, the board should move for a dismissal, "...for the good of the service." The matter was discussed, and the board expressed a consensus with Mr. Lloyd. After a short period of complete silence, Mr. Deaves spoke in a low voice, moving that the following resolution be adopted:

"RESOLVED: That for the good of the service Edward T. Hallissey be and he is hereby dismissed as Chief of Police of Haverford Township." The motion was seconded by Mr. Dewees, and quickly passed by a unanimous vote of the board.

The board then directed the secretary to write the following letter to Mr. Hallissey:

"Dear Sir:

I have to advise you that at a meeting of the Board of Commissioners held this day, you were dismissed for the good of the service, as Chief of Police of Haverford Township.

I was also instructed to request you to deliver to the undersigned as soon as practicable such papers, documents or other property which belong to the Township and which may be in your possession; also that you remove from the Township Building such property of your own as may be there.

Yours truly, (signed) H.A. Fritschman, Secretary"

So it was that Edward Hallissey was told that his law enforcement career was officially over, via a concise letter hand-delivered to his home. History does not record how the letter was received.

A newspaper article from 1913 begins, "Hallissey was thirty years old Monday a week ago, so he has before him a future with plenty of room for more glory." Sadly, that promising future was never fully realized.

The events following Hallissey's dismissal on April 11th 1921 seem almost anticlimactic. His hearing resumed on the 12th, and he was held for trial on all charges. It was December 22nd before his case was heard before Judge Gorman at Philadelphia City Hall. Hallissey entered a guilty plea to the charge of Operating an Automobile While Under the Influence of Liquor. Captain Smiley, Commander of the West Philadelphia Division who had been summoned to oversee Hallissey's arrest, appeared in court to speak on his behalf. Captain Smiley advised the judge, who was no doubt already aware, that Hallissey had lost his position as a result of his crime. He also advised the judge that Hallissey wasn't, "...a drinking man," and felt that with the approaching Christmas season, it would be a "nice thing" for any jail sentence to be suspended. Judge Gorman, in agreeing that a suspended sentence was called for, told Hallissey, "You are like a man who comes to the city all dressed up and slips on a banana peel."

Hallissey stayed in Haverford Township for the rest of his life. Two years after his dismissal, there was a brief flurry of public speculation that Hallissey was, "...planning a comeback." His successor as chief, former Philadelphia Detective-Lieutenant James Scanlin, had announced his impending resignation amid rumors that he was unhappy with political interference by the board. According to several Philadelphia papers, supporters of Hallissey seized the opportunity to circulate petitions urging the board to bring him back, and it was reported that several commissioners, including Edith Hannum, Pennsylvania's first female township commissioner, were favorably considering the possibility. The press blasted the very idea of Hallissey's return, and ran a series of stories highly critical of Hallissey and his reported campaign to "regain power." The entire affair was apparently a tempest in a teapot, based on rumors and spite. The board of commissioners publicly and vociferously denied even the remotest consideration of rehiring Hallissey, but the denials only served to stoke the fire. The stories continued apace until Hallissey wrote an impassioned appeal to the Upper Darby Herald, which was printed in an article headlined,

"AN OPEN LETTER FROM HALLISSEY."

For some time past my name has been persistently used in news stories from Haverford Township. The Philadelphia papers have that I am seeking the position held by Mr. Scanlin, and they have given me further undesirable publicity besides. For several years I have been trying to the best of my ability to live down a single mistake that I made. I am a tax payer in Haverford Township, and I do not see why I should be selected as the target for a lot of malicious lies. Even the most hardened criminal is given a chance in this modern age to live down his sins, but I have been selected as the one to be broken on the wheel.

I want to emphatically deny now that I ever wanted the Chief of Police job in Haverford Township if Scanlin resigned. If petitions have been circulated for me they have been circulated without my consent. I have a good paying position as it is, and no money would get me back as Chief of Police of Haverford Township.

All that I want is to be let alone to live my life as it suits me best. I am raising a family, and it is unfair to them as well as to myself, that I should be singled out for attack. I could hit back at my enemies if I wanted to, but I have refrained from doing so because I thought the people would forget me. All that I want you to do is to leave my name out of the paper entirely.

Sincerely yours,

EDWARD T. HALLISSEY

Oakmont, Del. Co., Pa.

Hallissey had found work as a regional representative for a Massachusetts shoe company. He and Lulu raised their family in their Ralston Avenue home, at some point moving to the nearby Southmore Court Apartments, where Hallissey died on February 21st, 1938. On the night of his death, he attended a testimonial dinner for County Sheriff William McKim at Brookline Country Club. The dinner was attended by 1,400 of the most influential Republicans of Delaware County, and was notable for seeing the launch of Judge Arthur James's successful gubernatorial campaign. Hallissey fell ill at the dinner, and was provided a ride home by a Haverford Police officer. His heart stopped within an hour of returning home. Edward Hallissey was just 54 years old.

Hallissey's spectacular fall from grace was national news. His high-profile career, coupled with the Spooner's Squire Scandal of 1919, made him an irresistible subject of headlines far and wide.

Left: Philadelphia Inquirer, April 8th 1921

Right: Washington Times, April 9th 1921

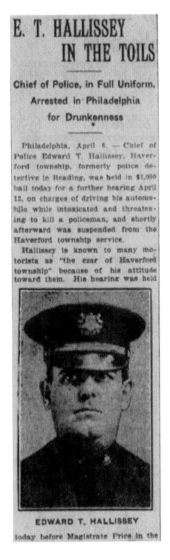

E. T. HALLISSEY
IN THE TOILS

Chief of Police, in Full Uniform, Arrested in Philadelphia for Drunkenness

Philadelphia, April 8. — Chief of Police Edward T. Hallissey, Haverford township, formerly police detective in Reading, was held in $1,000 bail today for a further hearing April 12, on charges of driving his automobile while intoxicated and threatening to kill a policeman, and shortly afterward was suspended from the Haverford township service.

Hallissey is known to many motorists as "the czar of Haverford township" because of his attitude toward them. His hearing was held today before Magistrate Price in the

EDWARD T. HALLISSEY

No news article could have been more embarrassing to Hallissey than this one, from the Reading Times edition of April 9th 1921. Hallissey had many friends and family in Reading, who were used to reading the positive stories that followed his career. They were likely shocked to see Hallissey's picture under the headline declaring him, "in the toils," a colorful period expression for someone behind bars.

Reading Times, April 9th 1921

HALLISSEY ARREST FREES INDIAN

Sioux's Name Inserted By Error in Copy of Charges Against Official

Philadelphia, April 14.— When "Chief" Rain-in-the-Face, a full-blooded Sioux Indian, failed to appear before Magistrate Price for a further hearing yesterday, following his arrest last week on a charge of firing arms within the city limits, it was learned that the Indian had gained his release on a copy of the charge issued in mistake for Edward J. Hallissey, former commander of the Haverford township police.

"Chief" Rain-in-the-Face was arrested last Friday, a few hours before "Chief" Hallissey was taken into custody.

The Indian chief was riding through the streets of West Philadelphia on an advertising campaign, dressed in full Indian regalia, when the police corraled him for firing blank cartridges in the air.

Both of the "chiefs" were in the station house at Sixty-first and Thompson streets at the same time, and when friends of "Chief" Hallis-

News of the bizarre mix-up that resulted in the release of "Chief Rain-in-the-Face" served as a fitting denouement to the non-stop coverage.

Reading Times, April 15th 1921

Hallissey's headquarters as it appears today, as viewed from the corner of Darby Road and Ralston Avenue. Hallissey lived a short distance away on Ralston Avenue. This structure, the original Haverford Township Building, remained police headquarters until 1929, when the department moved to Darby and Manoa Roads. The township administration offices rejoined the police department at the new Haverford Township Building, recently constructed at Darby and Manoa.

(Image from Google Earth Street View, used with permission.)

The scene of Hallissey's Philadelphia arrest as it looks today. Looking north on 60th Street from Market Street, under the tracks of the Market-Frankford Elevated Line. Hallissey drove onto the sidewalk where the arrow points in the center-right of the photo.

(Image from Google Earth Street View, used with permission.)

The Southmore Court Apartments at Benedict Avenue and Darby Road, where Edward Hallissey died on February 21st, 1938. In Hallissey's day, the tracks of the Ardmore and Llanerch Street Railway would traverse this scene left to right. Although now commonly considered a part of Oakmont, this neighborhood was known as South Ardmore for many decades.

(Image from Google Earth Street View, used with permission.)

Edward T. Hallissey, 1883-1938. 1st Chief of Police, Haverford Township.

He is buried at St. Denis Cemetery, Oakmont (Section 1, row 14).

<u>Epilogue</u>

One hundred years is a long time—that's one of the things I learned while writing this book. At the outset of this project, my goal was to write a short history of the Haverford Township Police Department, now celebrating a "Century of Service." But within a day or two of researching our first chief, I realized that Hallissey *was* the book. Although I have lived and worked in Haverford Township for almost a quarter-century, I knew next to nothing about Edward Hallissey before starting down this path. Sadly, I was not alone. As I discovered story after astounding story, I asked veteran and retired officers what they knew about Hallissey. None knew of his once-famous exploits with the State Police and in Reading. None knew of his amazing record of successful investigations and arrests. A few had heard something or other about the circumstances of his dismissal, but even that story had become muddled over the decades since his departure.

As I write this, steel columns are rising at the worksite near Darby and Manoa Roads that will soon become the new Haverford Township Building and police headquarters. I like to think that Hallissey would be proud of what "his" department has become. Seventy officers now patrol the same 10 square miles of Hallissey's day, but over the years, continued development has served to stitch together Haverford's various "towns." **(16)** The communities that make up the Township, once distinct enclaves connected by country roads, have grown into a continuous network of pleasant suburban streets, with a population of 50,000. As I drive the streets today, I can't help but gaze a bit longer at landmarks that remain from "Hallissey's Haverford." The old Township Building, always interesting to my eye, will now forever be Hallissey's headquarters. The Southmore Court Apartments, where quaint relics like built-in intercoms with separate ear and mouth-pieces remain, is even more interesting to me since I learned that Hallissey died there in 1938. I can't help but notice that from much of that building, on the corner of Darby and Benedict, one can look two blocks north and see the Township Building. I'll forever wonder if Hallissey chose an apartment that overlooked his old headquarters... (17)

I can't finish this book without addressing a question both simple and incredibly complex. What to make of Edward Hallissey? Is he a hero or villain? Cop's cop or rogue demagogue? Both? Neither? Any historical study must be conducted fully cognizant of the times in which the subject lived and breathed, and it's an understatement to say Hallissey lived in a different time. He rode with the 7th Cavalry and began his police career when horses were standard equipment. He was, in many ways, a product of his times. Life was hard. Police work was results driven—and Hallissey unquestionably got results.

It's difficult to reach back a century and extract meaningful tidbits that might serve to show a person's character, but some things did speak to me:

First—the people who were in a position to know him best liked him. He had friends. Reporters who added personal asides to or about him in their articles. Colleagues who choked-up when Hallissey roasted them while presenting a fraternal award. A commissioner from another township who didn't hesitate to bail him out when he learned of Hallissey's arrest. Real, true friends. Not to mention he still had the support of hundreds of residents; even after the incredible details of his arrest had been made known.

Second—Hallissey undoubtedly held the respect of those who worked for him and with him. The men who surprised him with an expensive gift. Two Philadelphia Police commanders, one a retired chief, who appeared in court to speak on his behalf. The chiefs who appointed him to their executive committee during his first year in their organization. In virtually every story written about Hallissey, and indeed there are many, his abilities and sense of command are unquestioned. He was, in today's terms, the real deal.

Third—Hallissey stayed. He could have disappeared with his family back to Reading or even Massachusetts, but didn't. He lived out his days within a few blocks of his old headquarters. He spent his last night among respected peers, toasting the county sheriff and the future governor of Pennsylvania. I believe that Hallissey lived by a code of honor, and paying for his mistake with his job satisfied the code. I'm fully convinced that he retracted his resignation not because he hoped to salvage his position; but rather, like a disgraced samurai who kneels before his Shogun awaiting the blade, he recognized that his transgression required that he face judgment rather than attempt to walk away.

I can't, and won't, attempt to justify Hallissey's conduct on April 7th 1921. But I'm fairly confident that he wouldn't want me to try. His actions speak for themselves. Officers Haase and Green were thrust into an impossible situation, and handled it as well as could be expected. If anything, Hallissey's sidewalk confrontation shows the impossibility of reasoning with someone who is drunk. And stipulating that he was drunk, it becomes perfectly believable that a man with Hallissey's life experience would reflexively clutch his blackjack and threaten violence when his alcohol-addled mind perceived an existential threat. I can only imagine how many times Hallissey later replayed that day in his mind--and how often he came to realize that at each turn, he did exactly the wrong thing.

One can only wonder what might have been. What fate might have had in store for Hallissey if only he had done things differently on that

April day. Could he have led his department for decades more, retiring with the praise and honor his career would have deserved? Or was his fall inevitable—the only end suitable for an anachronistic throwback as well-fitted to a progressive suburb as a bull to a china shop?   I prefer the former, but I'm admittedly biased. I started this project skeptical of Haverford's first chief. But the more I learned about Edward Hallissey, the more I found to like.   He was a complicated man who lived large during interesting times. I'm proud to know he was our first chief.

Several times during this project, I came close to shelving it.   I asked, what purpose does this serve? Am I doing a disservice by digging up things long past?   But in the end, I decided that Hallissey deserves to be remembered, that his story deserves to be told. If you've read this far, I thank you for allowing me to tell it.

Footnotes:

1. Today's popular "Pennsy Trail" recreation path, which runs between Manoa Road and the YMCA, is one of the few remnants of the rail line that allowed industry to flourish between Llanerch and Grassland. The location of the Grassland factories can be observed on the Mueller's Main Line Atlas. Descriptions of the Hall Concrete Company operations are found in period trade publications "Concrete" and "The Florists' Review." Details on the Essential Oils Specialties Company are found in "The American Perfumer and Essential Oil Review." Both companies regularly ran help-wanted ads in Philadelphia papers, advising potential employees to take an "Ardmore [trolley] car" (5 cents) from 69th Street to the Oakmont station, then walk the short distance to Grassland. The township's population centers were served by one or more station stops of the Philadelphia and West Chester (1895), Ardmore and Llanerch (1902), or Philadelphia and Western (1907) railways' trolley lines, with transfers possible at either Llanerch Junction or Ardmore Junction. The success of the trolleys caused the P.R.R. to discontinue passenger service on their branch line, but freight service into Haverford Township continued into the 1980's.

2. Constable Thompson worked as a police officer for the Philadelphia and West Chester Traction Company, protecting their properties and rolling stock from 69th Street to points west. He maintained an office, including a "lock-up," in the Traction Company's station at Llanerch Junction. Located near the point where the Pennsylvania Railroad crossed the tracks of the Philadelphia and West Chester trolley, the site of Constable Thompson's office is now a bus shelter on West Chester Pike adjacent to the Kohl's parking lot, across from Burger King. A careful observer can still note where the railroad crossed West Chester Pike, as the pavement has settled slightly and the relic of a signal's base remains in the median strip.

3. "Real Dime Novel Detective" is reprinted in the Appendix.

4. The annual "Chief's report" for 1914, as reported in the Reading Times of January 16th 1915, noted that Hallissey made 175 arrests that year.

5. Hallissey's quote is from the Reading Times of October 23rd 1915. Testimony of Fred Marks during his Disorderly Conduct hearing.

6. The temporary quarters of the police department was in an outbuilding on the property of George Deaves, a founding member of Oakmont Fire Company and one of the first township commissioners. His property, across from the High School (now Oakmont School), is currently the location of the Eagle Road Wawa. Oakmont Fire Company had offered to share their temporary quarters with the police department. Their stone firehouse on Darby Road would not be completed until 1919.

7. Archived historical copies of the commissioners' meetings minutes are viewable online at http://www.haverfordtownship.org/docs/archived-minutes

8. Ruins of the lake-house, a log-cabin built on the edge of the lake near the wooden dock, can still be found along the woods trail north of Marple Road, just west of the Quadrangle's small private golf course. It can be reached by following the Southbrook trail for one mile from the Haverford Reserve dog park. If one stands in front of the ruins and looks toward the distant treeline, the "bowl" of the lake can be discerned along the marsh grasses that surround the creek. The archives of the Haverford Township Historical Society include photos of the Allgates lake during happier times.

9. The difficulty in identifying Eddie Clark, also known as Fred Mickle a.k.a. Fred Johnson a.k.a. Joe Smith a.k.a. "Little Eddie" is typical of the problem of criminal identification faced by police agencies of the era. The FBI's Identification Division, a central records depository for fingerprints, would not be established until 1924. Until then, criminals could hope to evade justice by giving a

different name in each jurisdiction, as the patchwork system of identification relied on careful communication and cooperation.

10. An early 1920's development along the western boundary of the golf course, originally named "Golf View Road," was later renamed Furlong Avenue in honor of the beloved course superintendent who perished in the blaze.

11. If Hallissey did make such a boast, he was well on his way to seeing it through. A review of the treasurer's and finance committee reports in the commissioners' minutes for June of 1919 shows income from fines received the previous month totaled $1,469.00, while expenditures for the police payroll was $1012.50. The difference in the July 1919 report was even greater: $2,599.56 in fines received, with police payroll totaling $1,025.00.

12. Almost a hundred years later, residents give little mind to this remarkable sewer system, which thanks to regular inspection and maintenance performed by the Public Works Sewer crews, continues to perform its unseen yet vital function. Depending on location, each home's system connects to outfall lines that run along either Darby Creek or Cobbs Creek, to treatment plants in Southwest Philadelphia.

13. Some accounts spell the Officer's name as "Hasse." I have chosen to use the more common spelling. The 61st and Thompson Streets station house was then the home of the 29th Police District. District numbers have since been realigned, and it is now the 19th Police District. The building has since been rebuilt, and is also home to the Philadelphia Fire Department's Engine Company 41.

14. Details on the incident are mostly from contemporaneous accounts of court testimony.

15. The Corcorans were ultimately convicted and sentenced to two years at Eastern State Penitentiary. An article from the June 7th 1923 Inquirer, headlined "Convict Brothers View Body Of Their Mother," details how the brothers were brought to Llanerch from

the prison, and allowed to remain beside her coffin for 30 minutes while she lay in state at their home. "…They stood sobbing at the coffin of Mrs. Christine Corcoran; tried to comfort their sister, Harriet, and then were hurried back to prison by the two deputy wardens accompanying them. The brothers, Charles E. and Michael M. Corcoran, were convicted of stealing automobiles and sentenced to two years' imprisonment beginning May 16 last. They were not allowed to attend the funeral. Mrs. Corcoran died on Sunday, with the names of her boys on her lips, with a plea that they be brought to her."

16. The H.T.P.D., with an authorized strength of 70 sworn officers, is the third-largest department in Delaware County (after Upper Darby and Chester). In contrast to the hard-wired call-boxes of 100 years ago, their Delcom Sector 7 radio dispatches can be live-streamed via the Broadcastify website, at: https://www.broadcastify.com/listen/feed/20733

17. One thing is certain, Hallissey never referred to his neighborhood as "Havertown." That name was officially born on January 1st 1946 (eight years after his death), when 23 of Haverford Township's communities, previously served by the Llanerch Post Office, were designated as belonging to the newly created Havertown postal zone. The announcement, as reported in the January 2nd Philadelphia Inquirer, goes on to state: "The change, formulated several months ago, affects the following communities: Beechwood, Bon Air, Brookline, Chatham Village, Eagle Farms, Eagle Heights, Evergreen Estates, Greenview Park, Llanerch, Lynnewood Park and Manoa. Also affected are: Manoa Heights, Merwood, North Aronimink, Oakmont, Oakmont Park, Penfield, Richland Tract, South Ardmore, Upland Park, Westgate Hills, Westwood Park and Woodmere Park."

This un-credited article appeared in several papers, from Cincinnati to Mississippi, in July of 1913. Although some of the facts appear mildly embellished, most of the incidents are able to be cross-referenced with contemporary news accounts.

Real Dime Novel Detective

Sleuth That Has Had Many Thrilling Encounters With Desperate Criminals

[Philadelphia, North America]

Hallissey was 30 years old Monday a week ago. So he has before him a future with plenty of room for more glory. His work in Pennsylvania has been done during the last seven years. For six years previously he was in the Seventh and Forty-ninth United States Cavalry, and he saw active service in the Philippines and in the West. He quit the Constabulary 18 months ago to do detective work in Reading.

Hallissey was a lad of 17 when he enlisted from his home in Lynn, Mass; at the close of his army service he had attained the rank of Sergeant. He was in California with his regiment when he learned that a state constabulary was about to be formed in Pennsylvania, and he wrote to Captain Groome for an appointment. He came to Philadelphia for his final examinations, and was put on the "force."

He didn't know the meaning of fear. He was detailed on the more dangerous duties, and was finally made plainclothes man and assigned to all the big jobs that needed the services of a fearless man in Cumberland, Lehigh, Luzerne, Lebanon, Northampton, Columbia, Lackawanna, Berks, Chester and Philadelphia Counties.

He distinguished himself early in his constabulary duties by capturing notorious chicken thieves who had fooled Constables, Squires and police of various parts of the state. His first case was when two leaders of the "Chicken Gang" got away with eight or ten incubators and 1,000 eggs from a farmer at Fritztown. The theft was reported to Hallissey at 8 o'clock in the morning by Alderman Gerberich, of Allentown. By noon he found the men in a little hut, with the chickens boiling on the stove for dinner. The only evidence Hallissey had was that the name of the firm that had made the incubators was scratched on the bottom. He went to every farmhouse in the vicinity, examining the bottoms of the incubators until he found the right one. One man was convicted; but his pal, on the score of having a large family, was let off.

Shortly after this, Hallissey cleaned up the Welsh Mountain Gang, a notorious band of chicken thieves, by arresting their leader after a thrilling experience. Levi Shell was the bad man of the district. Farmers and Constables feared him, and when any attempts were made to arrest him, he usually shot the officer of the law. He was allowed to do as he pleased and went unmolested. After Shell had made a number of wholesale raids on the farmers in the north-western part of Lebanon county, Hallissey sent two of his men, Hollingsworth and Castner, to arrest him; he himself was due to testify in another case in Harrisburg. Hallissey was on the witness stand testifying when he received word that Shell had shot the two men, and reports had it at that time that they were both dying. Hollingsworth was shot through the cheek and Castner in the leg. Hallissey asked to be excused from the stand. Going directly to Lebanon, he took up the chase and followed the man for three days and three nights, finally locating him at hotel in Shellville, Dauphin County.

Shell was eating his supper in the dining room, with a loaded revolver on either side of his plate and 200 rounds of ammunition in his pockets. Hallissey sized up the situation at a glance. He saw that if he tried any sly means to get Shell unawares and failed, it would be all up with him. Although the dining room was a long one, Hallissey decided to face the man squarely from the front. He knew that the risk was a grave one; but it was the only chance. Hallissey, his revolver in his hand, rushed directly at his man. "Put up your hands!" he commanded.

Shell obeyed, but soon made several attempts to get the revolvers. Hallissey made him feel the cold steel against his temple, handcuffed him and threw the revolver to the floor. After he had securely fastened Shell to the chair, he emptied the revolvers, put them in his pocket, and relieved Shell of the 200 rounds of ammunition. He took Shell in the dead of night back to Lebanon, where he was tried and given nine years in the Eastern Penitentiary, for the wounded officers did not die.

This arrest made Hallissey a hero in the eyes of the farmers of Lebanon County. Testifying in Reading several years ago, when Hallissey had applied for a certificate as a private detective, Charles D. Weirick, The District Attorney of Lebanon County, said: "A number of farmers came to me and said that, when the bill was passed and signed by the Governor, they were greatly prejudiced against the state constabulary, but, after seeing Hallissey's work, they were strongly in favor of the constabulary, and felt amply protected when he was in their vicinity."

Hallissey distinguished himself again in Lebanon by his arrest of Michael Loncar, a Polander. Loncar was a desperate character. He had been in the Criminal Courts several times for making free use of his knife. His favorite drink was a mixture of beer and whiskey, and after getting a good dose of it he went to Shirk's Hotel, and, being refused a drink, proceeded to smash the bar and break the mirrors, windows and doors. When Mr. Shirk attempted to stop him, Loncar stabbed him.

Hallissey's headquarters were at the Wallace Hotel, in Lebanon. Receiving a phone call of the disturbance, he ordered a team and followed Loncar to a foreign settlement at Colebrook cinder bank. He learned that Loncar was in the attic of one of the houses. Opening the door, Hallissey found 30 of Loncar's friends in the house, ready to shield him. He demanded the fugitive. They told him that Loncar was in the attic, but dared the detective to get him. They said Loncar would not let him out alive.

Hallissey made his way up the narrow dark stairway to the attic room and seized his prisoner. The boldness of the arrest cowed Loncar for an instant, then, pulling out a long folding knife, he made a lunge at Hallissey. A desperate hand-to-hand fight followed between the two men, and Hallissey had to thump him with his blackjack. Taking him by the collar, Hallissey dragged Loncar down the steps and through his crowd of allies, who were too surprised to offer resistance. Putting him in the wagon, Hallissey sat on him and brought him to the police station at Lebanon. Then Hallissey realized for the first time that his wounds from Loncar's knife needed treatment, and he went to the hospital, where they were dressed.

Hallissey narrowly escaped with his life when he arrested Israel Patterson, alias James Patterson, now serving a term of 30 years in the Eastern Penitentiary on the evidence gained by Hallissey. Patterson, like Shell, was dreaded by the farmers in the mountain districts about Carlisle. He was a yeggman and had committed a series of robberies along the Pennsylvania Railroad. Among other crimes, he had held up an aged man and his daughter at the railroad station at Cockley, and, after tying and gagging the young woman and gagging the father, he blew open the safe and made off with its contents. Hallissey was detailed on the case. Disguising himself as a tramp, he spent several weeks in the open, begging his meals from place to place and getting his night's sleep wherever he could.

In this way Hallissey located Patterson's hut, two and a half miles east of Lee's Crossing, on the Shippensburg road. He asked for a bite to eat, and gained Patterson's confidence by telling him that he had "done a bit" in Philadelphia and escaped from jail.

Patterson and Hallissey became great friends. Patterson, who was an old man, with a large family of children and grandchildren, told the supposed tramp his entire life history. He recounted some jobs that he pulled off without getting caught, and the number of years he had spent in the "pen." Hallissey responded with narratives even more thrilling. When he was through "Old Man Pat" thought that he was even a worse citizen than he. Hallissey made his tale stronger by telling him of the various crooks he had met in the Eastern Penitentiary, many of whom were friends of Patterson. The old criminal didn't have a doubt that Hallissey was the "real thing," and wound up by telling him of the big "yegg" stunts and other crimes that he had engineered and laughed when he told how he had pulled the wool over eyes of authorities.

Unwittingly Patterson gave away all the secrets of the gang and made Hallissey a bona fide member, permitting him to assist in planning the new jobs. The old-time crook even took the sleuth through the mountains and showed him the different haunts of the gang.

When Hallissey found that he had enough evidence, he took advantage of his first opportunity to get away from Patterson to send a telegram to headquarters for assistance. Policeman Merrifield, with a squad of men, arrived at the hut at night, but Patterson had already had his suspicions aroused as to the identity of his guest and was prepared for such a situation. When the door of the hut opened with Hallissey and Merrifield in the lead, Patterson and his pals opened fire, seriously wounding Merrifield in the chest and arm. A fierce gun fight followed between the police and the outlaws. It was not until Hallissey fired a bullet into Patterson that the old man collapsed and gave in. He was taken to Carlisle and given the maximum penalty of 30 years in the Eastern Penitentiary.

Although Hallissey was an expert at disguise, he found that it was not so much fun as it looked on the surface. He often had to do hard manual labor in order to get a line on his man, and on one occasion worked in a mine for more than a week as a miner's laborer before he was able to convince himself that he was following the right man, by name Mike Nastico.

In this case all the description Hallissey had was that his man had a large scar on his right hand. Mike had fatally stabbed a fellow countryman in a fight over a girl in an Italian settlement in the upper part of Luzerne County. He fled to Scranton, where he lost no time in getting work as a miner. Hallissey followed him to the mine and secured a job as Nastico's assistant. He was not sure of his man, and there was not enough light in the shaft to see whether he had a scar on the back of his hand. He could not gain the fellow's confidence, for Nastico knew little English. One day he handed Hallissey a check on which to mark the number of the car. As he was handing back the check the sleuth felt the back of the Italian's hand, and next instant had a revolver at the man's head. He handcuffed Nastico's hand to his back and ordered the prisoner to lead the way out of the darkened shaft. There was not a man in hailing distance to whom Hallissey could appeal for assistance, and though he realized the risk he was taking in making the man a prisoner in a mine with which he was unfamiliar, he kept his nerve and wits about him. Along the entire passage through the shafts he let the Italian miner feel the steel of his revolver. Still wearing his miner's clothes, Hallissey took the man directly to Wilkesbarre. He is now serving 10 years in the Eastern Penitentiary.

Hallissey's most thrilling experience was the capture of Joe Chitshuck, who had committed an outrageous assault on a young girl, and fearing that her mother would give the alarm, shot and killed her, and then murdered the daughter. Then he went upstairs in the house and put on the father's clothes, which were too big for him, and left his own on the floor.

Hallissey was detailed on the case and traced Chitshuck from Merrivale to Orwigsburg, Schuylkill County, a distance of 200 miles, and thence to Reading, where Chitshuck registered at the City Hotel, and asked for the best room in the house. This was at 7 o'clock in the evening. Hallissey arrived at 5 o'clock the next morning, and finding that his man was at the hotel, went to his room and broke open the door. Chitshuck, who had taken his revolver to bed with him, fired as soon as the detective made his appearance, but fortunately for Hallissey, missed his aim. Hallissey blackjacked his man into submission, and later obtained a complete confession.

It is doubtful whether Hallissey was ever in a more ticklish position, or had a closer shave with death, than when he was in the cellar of a vacant house in Reading with a band of thieves known as the Emes Gang. A great number of mysterious robberies had occurred in Berks County. There were numerous yegg crimes along the Reading Railway; the post office at Reading was robbed and the home of William Sell, at Blandon, was ransacked. Hallissey was detailed on the case, and he felt sure that the same gang had committed all of the robberies.

A number of reports were received along the railroad tracks that the signals were being tampered with, and Hallissey soon found that the robbers were causing that trouble, too. One of the men wore a peculiar heelplate on his shoe, and Hallissey noted the marking of this plate on every shoe print identified with the crime.

Hallissey finally traced the gang to a house on Ninth street, Reading. He got into the cellar and listened to them talking over their deeds and planning the next job. In the early morning he went out to give an alarm and to have the house surrounded. When he returned to his hiding place he found that George Emes, a character who was feared by the police, was hiding behind a pile of boards. Hallissey fired to frighten the man, and Emes fired back. Hallissey fell over as if dead. The trick proved most successful. Emes came out of his hiding place, and he was bending over the supposed dead man when Hallissey snapped the handcuffs on him.

The sound of the shots attracted the men who were upstairs. Hallissey was fearlessly facing a battle with them when the police arrived and helped him take the gang into custody. Jeremiah Rishel and Harry Emes were given nine years on charges of highway robbery, burglary and larceny. George Emes pleaded guilty without standing trial and was given two and a half years. Emes has served his term, and according to Hallissey, who keeps in constant touch with him, he is living down his past and is doing well.

Appendix B:
Excerpts from the archived minutes of the Haverford Township Board of Commissioners meeting, June 5th 1916.

Mr. Moore introduced and the President read an Ordinance, entitled, "AN ORDINANCE TO ESTABLISH A NIGHT WATCH AND POLICE FORCE IN AND FOR THE TOWNSHIP OF HAVERFORD AND TO PRESCRIBE THE DUTIES OF THE SAME AND TO PROVIDE FOR THE SALARIES OF POLICE OFFICERS", which Ordinance was referred to the Ordinance Committee and by it favorably reported. On motion of Mr. Dewees, seconded by Mr. Deaves, and duly passed, that the Ordinance be adopted as read, the Board proceeded to the adoption of the Ordinance, and upon roll call, the vote standing, Ayes, Messrs. Cooke, Cunningham, Deaves, Dewees, Lloyd and Moore, Noes, none, the Ordinance was declared adopted in the following form:-

(NO. 77).

AN ORDINANCE

TO ESTABLISH A NIGHT WATCH AND POLICE FORCE IN AND FOR THE TOWNSHIP OF HAVERFORD AND TO PRESCRIBE THE DUTIES OF THE SAME AND TO PROVIDE FOR THE SALARIES OF POLICE OFFICERS.

The Board of Commissioners of Haverford Township, Delaware County, Pennsylvania, do ordain:-

SECTION 1. That a night watch and police force shall be and is hereby established and that the same shall consist of a Chief of Police and not more than nine Policemen, one of whom may be appointed Sergeant of Police'

The Chief of Police shall be appointed by the Board of Commissioners and shall not be removed except for inefficiency,

incapacity, insubordination and conduct unbecoming an officer.
Further, that the Police Committee will be empowered to suspend
the Chief of Police for a period not exceeding thirty (30) days
and that the Board of Commissioners may continue suspension for
such longer time, or removal, as it may deem proper, when in their
opinion the Chief of Police has been found guilty of inefficiency,
incapacity, insubordination, or conduct unbecoming an officer.

One Sergeant and eight Policemen shall be appointed by the
Board at any time, or from time to time, as public necessity shall
require and shall not be removed except for inefficiency, incapacity
insubordination, or conduct unbecoming an officer, as hereinafter
provided. All officers under this Ordinance shall become residents of the Township and their appointment shall be in writing
and shall take effect only upon such officers taking and sub-
scribing an oath or affirmation before a Justice of the Peace to
faithfully perform every duty incumbent upon them under the laws
of this Commonwealth and Ordinances and Regulations of the Township of Haverford.

SECTION 3. The Chief of Police shall receive a salary of
not more than One hundred and twenty-five dollars ($125.) per
month; the Sergeant shall receive a salary of not more than
Eighty dollars ($80.) per moth, and Policemen shall receive a
salary of not more than Seventy dollars ($70.) per month. The
Township shall provide and each officer shall wear at all times
while on duty, a uniform of dark gray cloth of a pattern and
style prescribed by the Police Committee, together with an

appropriate badge and such other equipment as the said Committee
shall prescribe.

SECTION 3.   The Police Committee of the Board of Commissioners
shall have the power to prescribe the duties of the officers to be
appointed under this Ordinance and to make all necessary Police
Rules and Regulations, subject to the provisions thereof and subject also to be modified or approved by the Board of Commissioners.

SECTION 4.   It shall be the duty of the Chief of Police to
be the chief executive officer of the Police Department.   It shall
be his especial duty to repair promptly to all serious fires and
to all riots and tumultuous assemblages within the Township,
to take command of the police there present, to save and protect
property, to disperse mobs, and to arrest or cause to be arrested
all persons disturbing the public peace, or inciting others there-
to; also to enforce or assist in the enforcement of the Health
Regulations of the Township; and generally to perform such other
duties as may be required of him by the Ordinances and Police Regulations of the Township and the laws of the Commonwealth.   The
Chief of Police shall be responsible for the efficiency and discipline of the police force.   The Chief of Police shall have the
authority by and with the consent of the Police Committee to
appoint special officers in case of necessity, for not exceeding
five days, at not exceeding two dollars and fifty cents per day.

SECTION 5.   The Chief of Police shall keep or cause to be
kept an official docket in which shall be recorded all arrests,

by whom made, or causes therefor and the disposition of the
arrested parties. An abstract of said docket shall be submitted, together with a report to the Police Committee at least
two (2) days before each regular monthly meeting of the Board of
Commissioners.

SECTION 6. The Sergeant and Policemen shall render the most
implicit obedience to the orders of the Chief of Police. Policemen shall patrol their respective beats during all of the time
they are on duty and shall be governed in making arrests of
all drunken, disorderly and suspicious persons by the laws of
this Commonwealth, and by the Ordinances and Regulations of the
Township. It shall also be the duty of the Policemen to inspect
the street lights maintained by the Township and to immediately
report any lights not in good order and further to inspect all
poles, lines and overhead wires and all streets and roads con-
taining water, gas or other pipe-lines and to immediately report
any defects therein or dangerous condition caused thereby, to the
Board of Commissioners and the Chief of Police shall report semi-
annually in writing to the Board of Commissioners upon the condition of all such poles, lines, pipes and wires.

SECTION 7. The Police Committee shall have the authority,
in the temporary absence of the Chief or any officer from duty,
to appoint a substitute, if necessary, who shall have the same
powers and the same privileges as the regular officer of such
rank may have, during the absence of such officer, or until
another appointment shall be made. Provided, That such substitute shall receive only the compensation that would otherwise

be due the regular officer whose substitute he is.

SECTION 8. The Chief of Police shall have the authority to suspend any subordinate without pay for inefficiency, incapacity, insubordination, or conduct unbecoming an officer, such suspension to take effect immediately and to continue for such a period not longer than thirty days, as the Chief of Police shall prescribe; provided that report of such suspension shall be made at the next regular meeting of the Board of Commissioners. The Board of Commissioners may continue such suspension, at its discretion, for such longer time as it may deem proper. No subordinate officer shall be discharged except by the Board of Commissioners when in the opinion of the Board such officer is inefficient, incapable, insubordinate or guilty of conduct unbecoming an officer. No officer appointed hereunder shall at any time while in the employment of the Township take any part in politics, and any officer who shall so participate shall be immediately suspended and discharged.

Approved by the Board of Commissioners this Fifth day of June, A. D. 1916.

_____
Horatio ~~~~~~
President.

Attest: _____
Horace B Moore
Secretary.

Mr. Moore, Chairman of the Police & Fire Committee, reported as follows:-

"We ask the appointment of the following men for Police

76

Duty, if they pass examinations, subject to the Chief's
approval: George T. Neeley, Ardmore; William Compton,
Llanerch; Harry Grove, Preston; John Glacklin, Preston; Eugene
Graney, Oakmont."   On motion of Mr. Dewees, seconded by Mr.
Deaves and duly passed, the vote standing, Ayes, Messrs. Cooke,
Cunningham, Deaves, Dewees, Lloyd and Moore, Noes, none, it was
Resolved that the report be received and the recommendations
adopted.

A letter from the Brookline Fire Company referring to certain
police powers of Firemen, was referred to the Committee on Police
& Fire.

On motion of Mr. Deaves, seconded by Mr. Cunningham and
duly passed, the vote standing, Ayes, Messrs. Cooke, Cunningham,
Deaves, Dewees, Lloyd and Moore, Noes, none, it was Resolved
that the Township add to its contract with the Counties Gas &
Electric Company, three lights to be located as follows: one
at Hirst & Florence Avenues, one at Pennfield & Merion Avenues,
andone at Wexford & Kenmore Roads.

Mr. Deaves was requested by the Board to procure a map of
the Township showing the locations of all Lights and Fire
Hydrants.

On motion of Mr. Deaves, seconded by Mr. Dewees and duly
passed, the vote standing, Ayes, Messrs. Cooke, Cunningham,
Deaves, Dewees, Lloyd and Moore, Noes, none, it was Resolved that
a Committee of three be appointed to draft an Ordinance embodying
building restrictions for buildings within the Township.

Mr. Dewees introduced and the President read an Ordinance, entitled, "AN ORDINANCE TO AUTHORIZE THE MAKING OF A TEMPORARY LOAN OF FIVE THOUSAND DOLLARS, OR PART THEREOF FOR THE PURPOSE OF PAYING FOR REAL ESTATE FOR TOWNSHIP BUILDING, FOR HAVERFORD TOWNSHIP, DELAWARE COUNTY, PENNSYLVANIA, AND APPROPRIATING THE SAID SUM TO SUCH ACCOUNT," which Ordinance was referred to the Ordinance Committee and by it favorably reported. On motion of Mr. Deaves, seconded by Mr. Moore and duly passed, that the Ordinance be adopted as read, the Board proceeded to the adoption, and upon roll call, the vote standing, Ayes, Messrs. Cooke, Cunningham, Deaves, Dewees, Lloyd, and Moore, Noes, none, the Ordinance was declared adopted in the following form:-

(NO. 78).

AN ORDINANCE

TO AUTHORIZE THE MAKING OF A TEMPORARY LOAN OF FIVE THOUSAND DOLLARS, OR PART THEREOF FOR THE PURPOSE OF PAYING FOR REAL ESTATE FOR TOWNSHIP BUILDING, FOR HAVERFORD TOWNSHIP, DELAWARE COUNTY, PENNSYLVANIA, AND APPROPRIATING THE SAID SUM TO SUCH ACCOUNT.

The Board of Commissioners of Haverford Township, Delaware County, Pennsylvania, do ordain:

FIRST. That the sum of Five thousand dollars, or such part thereof as may be deemed necessary, be borrowed for the purpose of paying for the tract of ground, the purchase of which was authorized by the Board of Commissioners on May 10th, 1915, and the said sum of Five Thousand Dollars is hereby appropriated to the account of Township Building.

SECOND. That the President and Secretary of the Board be authorized, empowered and instructed to make such note or notes, not exceeding in the aggregate the sum of Five Thousand Dollars, as in their judgment be deemed necessary and to borrow thereon from such banks, trust companies or persons as they may deem best, at a rate of interest not to exceed six per cent per annum.

Approved by the Board of Commissioners this fifth day of June, one thousand nine hundred and sixteen.

_____
                              President.

Attest: _____
                    Secretary.

On motion duly made, seconded and carried the meeting adjourned.

_____
                    Secretary.

ABOUT THE AUTHOR

Albert "Matt" Hufnal is a detective and 25-year veteran of the Haverford Township Police Department. Prior to joining the HTPD, he was an officer with the Metro Transit Police Department in Washington D.C. During his enlistment in the Marine Corps, he served as a squad leader with the security detail for HMX-1, the "Marine One" helicopter squadron. Matt lives in Haverford Township with his wife, son, and daughter. This is his first book.

Made in the USA
Columbia, SC
05 May 2018